Kendall Antosh

BRIDE on a MISSION™

Wedding Workbook for the CRAFTY, the THRIFTY, & the FEISTY Bride-to-Be

ISBN-13: 978-1518753701
ISBN-10: 1518753701

Bride on a Mission
www.BrideonaMission.net

Printed by CreateSpace
www.CreateSpace.com/5820514

For my girls.

There is nothing you can't do.

ACKNOWLEDGMENTS

My very sincere thanks to the couples who trusted me enough to test-drive this book as they planned their weddings. Thank you to my friends and family who were willing to read and edit my rough drafts, especially my mom, who is my biggest cheerleader. Most of all, thank you to my husband, who never doubted me, not even once.

Contents

This text is written in a voice that addresses a bride who is planning a wedding with her groom. Every couple is beautifully unique, and so please take the wording with a grain of salt. It is not meant to exclude anyone. If you find yourself in very different circumstances, I believe the lists, worksheets, and ideas within these pages can be relevant and effective when you apply them to your own beautifully unique event.

Also, this book contains advice and information relating to the planning of weddings. It includes mentions of relationship dynamics, sanity, and counseling. It is not intended to substitute for medical or psychological diagnosis and treatment. This text should be used as a supplement to - not substitute for - any relationship counseling or marriage preparation recommended or prescribed to you and your fiancé.

INTRODUCTION:
becoming a
BRIDE on a MISSION

What kind of Bride on a Mission are you?

The Crafty Bride:
a D.I.Y.* diva who owns more pairs of scissors than pairs of shoes. She likes to learn a new skill with each project.

The Thrifty Bride:
she knows how to plan and where to spend, saving both time and money. Her big day will be rich with what matters most to her.

The Feisty Bride:
she likes to be in control and maybe a little irreverent. She's determined to have a blast as she plans her wedding.

*Do It Yourself

What is a Bride on a Mission made of? Determination, grace, and sass. She is both in control and flexible. She is sometimes crafty, a little thrifty, and not afraid to be feisty. Your mission, should you choose to accept it, is this: plan your wedding, make it uniquely your own, and have fun!

This mission may change you. It begins with a ring and a question, and it ends when you become someone's spouse. Along the way, you will have opportunities to morph into a Bridezilla. With preparation, perspective, and poise, you can become a Bride on a Mission instead.

Preparing to walk down the aisle may be the biggest project of your life. That's because there are a lot of things that go along with that aisle. No one will blame you if you get overwhelmed. There will be roadblocks. Things never go 100% as planned. It's okay to get frustrated. Unless you are on reality TV, suppress the urge to freak out and burn bridges.

Reality check! In order to officially have a wedding, you NEED the following: two consenting adults (preferably in love), a marriage license, an officiant, and witnesses. Everything else is tradition and fads. When it's over, you are just as married as anyone else.

To plan a wedding yourself, it does not mean that you have do every single job yourself. Get help from the people who love you, but without testing the limits of their love. When you hire a vendor (or contractor) for a task, time is money. You can save both time and money if you equip yourself with the tools in this book, plus you can have fun too!

The Planning Mindset

Even the most organized Bride can feel caught up in a whirlwind of lace, monograms, and wedding blogs. To get into the planning mindset, first find a little notebook that you can keep with you everywhere. Inspiration can strike at any time, and good advice can come from anyone you meet. In that notebook, your on-the-spot wedding ideas are all in one place. Plus, you will not need a perfect memory to keep it all straight. Use your inspiration notebook to:

- Take notes: ideas, epiphanies, advice (good & bad), and anything you may forget after your next margarita
- Make lists (see the *List of Lists*, opposite)
- Scrapbook pictures that you like from magazines
- Practice signing your married name

Questions about your wedding plans are inevitable. It's time to mentally prepare with answers. Even if you have been engaged for three minutes, people will immediately ask, "Have you set a date?" and then grill you about your wedding plans. It can drive you crazy, but it's okay to have zero plans! Practice saying things like, "I'm touched that you are so excited, but it's too soon to know what flavor the wedding cake will be."

Also prepare for the onslaught of unsolicited advice and suggestions. Practice saying, "Thank you for the idea. When the time comes to make a decision about my 'something blue', I'll keep your rhinestone tiara in mind." For a little extra oomph!, add the following, "In fact, let me write that down so I don't forget!" and whip out the notebook mentioned above.

The Checklist (how it works and how to use it)

Since your engagement can be any length of time, the items in The Checklist (opposite) are grouped by phases. You may also notice that with some of the big action items, there are related decisions listed below. Not everything has to be done at the same time! The deadline is the wedding day, after all.

Sit down with your fiancé to decide which items on The Checklist you would like to do together, which tasks you will pawn off on someone else, and divvy up the rest between you. Set some deadlines for the big stuff. The caterer, photographer, florist, wedding coordinator/planner, and venues are going to be the first things you need to book, so you get the ones you want. They are also going to be the biggest money pits. To see how the cost factor will drive your wedding plans, see the Budget section (page 10).

We Just Got Engaged - Now What?

- ❑ **Announce** your engagement as formally or informally as you like; there are no rules these days.
- ❑ **Celebrate** getting engaged! Do so in a way that will set the tone of your engagement and your wedding planning. An upcoming wedding is something to be joyful about, even if you have been married before or if you happen to be knocked up.
- ❑ **Rings**. Get your engagement ring sized. If you don't like the ring, now is the time to say so, but say so nicely. (Hint: a good compromise is to use the stone(s) in an different setting, like in a family heirloom). This ring will be on your hand for the rest of your life, after all.
  - ❑ Select your wedding rings. (Hint: many retailers offer layaway).
  - ❑ Insure all of your rings and ask about a resizing costs / programs available.
  - ❑ Get your wedding rings engraved and sized.
- ❑ **Prepare to plan**. Get an inspiration notebook, a folder for paperwork, and access to the internet (Hint: bridal magazines and public computers are often available at the library). Set aside special time for browsing, reading, and sorting through all of your options.
- ❑ **Consider others' vision**. Chat with your fiancé and each of your parents about their wedding day *must-haves* before you set anything in stone.

The Foundation

- ❑ **Budget**. This is a big decision: how much do you want to spend? Ask both sets of your parents (or other special people) if they are willing to contribute to the wedding (either a dollar amount, a percentage of the total, or specific expenses). The Shopping List can help you anticipate all possible expenses (Hint: just because you make something yourself does not mean it will be cheap).
- ❑ **Bridal Party**. Ask (don't tell) your brides-maids, groomsmen, flower girl, ring bearer, and VIPs if they will take part in your wedding. Let them know what the job entails (see page 82). If someone declines, be cool with it.
- ❑ **Location**. Pick a city for the festivities. The old tradition is to use the Bride's home town.
- ❑ **Venues**. Decide if you want the wedding & reception to be at the same venue or at two separate venues. Research potential venues, noting their pricing and available dates.

THE LIST OF LISTS

Wedding Party & VIPs
Guest List
The Checklist (on pages 3-9)
Shopping List (on pages 12-16)
Gift Registry (see page 85 for help)
Vendors' Contact Information
Flower Distribution (see page 40)
Helpers & descriptions of their jobs
Order of Events / Schedule
Ceremony Songs & Cues
Reception "Must-Play" Song List
Reception "Do-Not-Play" Song List
Must-Have Photos (see page 62)
Group Photos
Emergency Kit (see page 77)
Name Change Notification List

continued →

The Foundation (continued)

- ❑ **The Date**. Sit down with your fiancé and a calendar to choose a few possible wedding dates. If the date is flexible, then do the following:
  - ❑ Tell your parents, wedding party, and VIPs about your possible dates and ask them to "speak now or forever hold your peace." Give them some time to check their calendars and veto any dates.
  - ❑ Cross reference the remaining possible dates with the places that you have in mind for the wedding venue and the reception venue. If the stars align, then set the date!

- ❑ **Vendors**. Decide what level of help you want for each job. If you want to hire a vendor (someone paid and under contract) for a task, start doing your research, get referrals from your recently married friends, and speak to the person in charge (Hint: each chapter of this book includes discussion topics for those conversations).

- ❑ **Tradition**. Decide on the wedding tradition/culture/ religion that you will celebrate. Research everything that goes along with it.
  - ❑ Find out it you will need to provide your own fixtures (like an altar, unity candle, sand ceremony, canopy, chuppah, or manddap) in order to observe your tradition/culture/religion within the venue.
  - ❑ Look for a retailer or renter for the traditional fixtures.

- ❑ **Theme**. Picture your attire and décor in the setting of your venue. More on page 34.
  - ❑ What is the overall look and feel (i.e. royal, western, modern, Vegas, shabby chic, nautical)?
  - ❑ Pick two or three colors for your theme (in addition to black and white), or even a pattern.
  - ❑ Picture how you might reverently decorate the traditional fixtures to match your theme.

- ❑ **Bridal Show**. Find out when the next bridal show will be in your area and put it on your calendar.

- ❑ **Marriage Prep**. Enroll in a marriage preparation program: online, at your place of worship, with a counselor, or through your city/state.

❑ Get Help(ers) SOME EXAMPLES ARE:

Crafty Helper is your guide or sidekick with DIY projects in the planning phase.

Ceremony Setup Helpers know how and where to put the traditional fixtures, sign-in table, flowers, chairs, altar, and décor (possibly in your absence).

Reception Setup Helpers know how and where to put the tables & chairs, place settings, centerpieces, specialty tables, photo booth, and other décor (possibly in your absence).

Vendor Wrangler needs to be at the reception site during set up and again just before the guests arrive, making sure the vendors arrange their tables according to plan. This person must be trusted to make on-the-spot decisions.

Flower Distributor gets each bouquet, corsage, and boutonniere with the right person and properly pinned, if necessary.

Kid Jockey keeps flower girls and ring bearers together and entertained before the ceremony.

Greeter hands out ceremony programs.

Ushers seat your guests as they arrive at the ceremony. They officially begin the ceremony by seating the grandparents and parents.

Readers take part in the ceremony by reading a poem, scripture, or passage.

Wedding Gown Helper will button/zip/lace up the wedding gown, bustle the train for the reception, and help the Bride go pee. The day after the wedding, she will pick up the gown from the Bride and take it to safety.

Dressing Room Steward will make sure the bridal party leaves nothing behind. This person could also be in charge of the emergency kit, Bridal Party purses, and the marriage license.

Getaway Car Chauffeur drives the couple to the reception, and brings the getaway car up to the front door in time for the grand exit.

Takedown Helpers pack up your stuff, clean up, and stack chairs after the reception.

Rental Steward returns all the rented items while you depart for your Honeymoon.

You Are Cordially Invited

❏ **Wedding Website**. These are free to set up through major wedding sites. Use the web to keep your guests informed.

❏ **Guest List**. Start collecting addresses from friends and family. (Hint: ask recently married/graduated relatives for their address lists as a starting point). In the early stages, plan for about two-thirds of your invitees to attend.

❏ **Save-The-Dates**. Once you have made a list of your guests, let them know the date and the city of your wedding. Share your wedding website address. If you have already selected guest accommodations and/or arranged for a group discount, include that information as well.

❏ **Gift Registry**. Guests like to bring gifts. A registry tells your guests exactly what you want. If you don't make a registry, you will end up with a collection of non-returnable Elvis dinner plates. See page 85 for some ideas.

  ❏ Envision how you want to decorate your future home.

  ❏ Have an argument with your fiancé. Why if you both already own everything you need, do you need to register for more stuff? Why not just ask for cash? The answer is that most of your guests will want to bring a wrapped gift. Besides, he can register for tools and tech gadgets.

  ❏ Register at two to four retailers, with at least one available online. Update your registry often. More on page 85.

  ❏ Register at a spa or a lingerie store… for the feisty gift-givers. Maybe don't mention this one on your website.

  ❏ Let your bridal shower hostess and your wedding website spread the word about your gift registries. Never mention your gift registries in your wedding invitation.

❏ **Invitations**. Thumb through examples (online or in a store) to help you choose the style, wording, and design. Incorporate your theme & colors. Include an RSVP cutoff date. Mail the invitations four to eight weeks before the big day. Consider ordering other stationery in the same motif. More on page 20.

❏ **Get Fit**. Adopt a physician-approved exercise and eating plan that you can commit to from this day forward. Give yourself a pass to break your diet any time someone throws you a party.

❏ **THE Dress**. Start designing or shopping for your wedding gown. See page 46. Some retailers do not sell off the rack and require a few months to make and alter their pieces. (Hint: Your bridal portrait session is the due date). For a custom gown, find a seamstress or get sewing.

❏ **Officiant**. Decide who will preside over your wedding ceremony. This may be a priest, minister, justice of the peace, ship's captain, or someone who has been certified online.

  ❏ If you want an officiant who is not associated with your place of worship, verify that an outside officiant is allowed.

  ❏ If you don't have an officiant, start your research. Conduct phone interviews or meet with your candidates to get a feel for their style.

  ❏ Meet with the officiant to sign your contract, get ideas for the Ceremony order of events, discuss what (s)he might say during the Ceremony, and make a plan for the microphone (more on page 74).

  ❏ Write or choose your vows.

HELPFUL SEARCH TERMS

Free Wedding Website
Registry Ideas
Wedding Dress Size Chart
Reception Drink Calculator
Wedding Vows
Online Marriage Prep
Invitation Wording
Flower in Season
Wedding Seating Chart Maker
Reception Schedule

continued →

Planning the Party

❏ **Browse**. Pre-screen vendors online. Look for upcoming events (like a tasting or open house) that you can attend.

❏ **Flowers**. Envision your bouquets, altar flowers, boutonnieres, corsages, centerpieces, and archways before you meet with a florist. (Hint: incorporate fake flowers and inanimate objects, not just fresh flowers). More on page 40.

❏ **Décor**. Plan with your quantities in mind because every décor decision gets multiplied out many times. If you find a fabulous item that you want to use, and you would need a few dozen, make sure you can get that many in time.

❏ **Food**. Choose a caterer or Helper(s) for the reception food preparation and service. Plan your number of courses and menu items, including a vegetarian option and a kid's option.

❏ **Booze**. Decide if you will have self-serve beverages or a bartender. Plan how you will stock the bar (see page 68).

❏ **Cake**. Research bakeries and get an idea how you would like your wedding cake and Groom's cake (or other dessert) to look and taste. (Hint: grocery stores have bakeries that are affordable and consistent in quality).

❏ **Honeymoon**. Research travel packages online or contact a travel agent. Apply for passports if necessary. Groom: if the destination is a secret, at least tell the Bride what climate to pack for. Get travelers checks, if appropriate.

❏ **Bridal Party Attire**. Pick out what you want the bridesmaids, groomsmen, flower girls, ring bearer and VIPs to wear and how their colors will coordinate. If you are making them pay for their attire, keep it low-cost or re-wearable (Hint: shiny satin dresses are not re-wearable outside of prom).

❏ **Hair and Makeup**. First, decide if you want to hire stylists or do your hair or makeup yourself. (Hint: invest in waterproof mascara, long-lasting makeup, and some serious hair spray. Test-drive them often. Avoid liquid makeup that you will have to apply/re-apply while wearing your wedding dress).

   ❏ Decide on your hair style and how you would like to incorporate a veil, tiara, combs, barrettes, extensions, etc.

   ❏ Research hair stylists. Look at photos of their work and get prices for a bridal hairdo or a hair/makeup package (Hint: ask for a volume discount on getting hair & makeup done for your bridesmaids, moms, and flower girls).

   ❏ Sign a contract with your hair stylist & makeup artist and schedule a trial run. (Hint: have your trial run on the day of your bridal portraits or the day of your bridal shower).

   ❏ Splurge on a beauty treatment like teeth whitening, laser hair removal, microderm abrasion, or backne medicine.

   ❏ Set up appointments for you and the bridesmaids to get manicures & pedicures for the day before the wedding (Hint: set the time so that it is the last thing you do before the rehearsal, to reduce the risk of chipped nails).

❏ **Photography**. No matter who takes the wedding photos, this person MUST have experience. Taking photos of mountains is not the same as taking photos of hungry herds of wedding guests. A good photographer is not necessarily a good wedding photographer. Evaluate the photographer's body of work, as well as their personality.

❏ **Music**. Get your music plan in order for both the ceremony and the reception. Will you use a DJ, band, string quartet, cantor, or a Helper (to press PLAY and PAUSE at the right times)? Start taking dance lessons or choreographing your viral-video-worthy dance moves.

❏ **Transportation**. Rent a limo/horse drawn carriage/classic car for your wedding-day transportation. If you use your own car or borrow a vehicle, designate a Helper to take the getaway car to get washed and detailed.

❏ **Be Generous**. Get gifts for your Bridal Party and Helpers. (Hint: leftover reception booze is a legit Helper gift).

❑ Communicate

With your Maid of Honor and Best Man. What do you want out of your bridal shower (what city, which guests, what kind, and how many showers)? What are the ground rules for the bachelor & bachelorette parties? Who gets to say a toast and at which event? Who will give the vendors their tips?

With your Bridal Party. What events do they need to attend, and where can they stay? Will they help set up & take down the ceremony and reception? Explain or diagram how they will stand during the ceremony and receiving line.

With your Helpers. Let your ushers know what ushering looks like and how the order of seating for important family members. Readers will need to know what they will be reading and when in the schedule it happens.

With your parents. Let them know if you need more or less of their involvement. Who gets to give a toast and at which event? Who will handle the wedding gifts after the reception and where will they take them? Give them a copy of the honeymoon itinerary in case of an emergency.

With your guests. If your guests will have to pay for anything along the way (cash bar, tolls, valet, or a parking fee), they need to know in advance.

With your employer. Ask your boss for the time off that you will need. (Hint: include the day before the wedding and the day after the honeymoon).

❑ **Guest Accommodations**. Decide whom will be allowed to stay in your house and then get a group rate at a hotel for everyone else. (Hint: choose a hotel close to the reception venue so your guests have a short distance to drive at the end of the night). Book any rooms that you will be paying for.

❑ For a small guest list or a hard-to-find venue, consider pre-paying for shuttle service. Your guests can travel between hotel and venues without getting lost, arriving late, or driving drunk.

❑ Put together baskets for the venue restrooms with items that your guests can use to freshen up. Consider a welcome gift for out-of-state guests .

❑ **Party Hearty**. Let your bridal party or a member of your extended family host a bridal shower in your honor. Let your friends throw you a bachelorette party. (Hint: you decide how wild is too wild. Also, let your friends help you stock up on lingerie for the honeymoon).

❑ **Schedule**. Find out when the doors will be unlocked to your venues and make a schedule for the rehearsal day, wedding day, day after, and the honeymoon. (Hint: On the wedding day, focus on the order of the events, not an exact time you expect each event to happen. More on page 74).

After the RSVP Cutoff Date

❑ **Guest List.** Call anyone who has not responded to the wedding or rehearsal dinner invitations and ask for their answer. Sometimes invitations get lost, and sometimes people are clueless about etiquette.

❑ **Caterer.** Give your caterer the final headcount. Your final balance may change (Hint: give your caterer the actual headcount, since it is their job to make sure that there is enough food). Confirm their part of the schedule.

❑ **Seating**. Create a seating chart. Make place cards & table numbers.

❑ **Tables**. Update the quantities of tables, chairs, place settings, etc. with your rental company/caterer/venue. Confirm the time that the items will be ready for pickup or when they will be delivered. (Hint: rental companies may penalize you for waiting too long to make these updates).

❑ **Flowers**. Update the quantity of centerpieces, bouquets, boutonnieres, and corsages with the florist. Confirm the time that the flowers will be delivered/ready for pickup. Update your Flower Helper's list.

❑ **Booze**. Order the Champagne, beer, wine, alcohol, and mixers.

❑ **Parking**. Arrange for the volume of cars that you are expecting. (Hint: plan for one vehicle for every two guests).

❑ **Kids**. Make some kind of entertainment available for your little guests, like coloring books. If you want them to be separate from the main party, then hire a babysitter and set aside a nearby area where kids can be contained. (Hint: be cool with it if parents choose not to utilize such a service).

continued →

One Week to Go

Marriage License
Office Research:
- fees & available discounts
- required legal items (i.e. photo IDs, divorce decree from a previous marriage, and proof of prep course)
- hours of operation

❑ **Marriage License**. Take an afternoon off of work and go with your fiancé to get your marriage license. Government offices are usually closed on the weekend.

❑ **Officiant**. Meet with the officiant to go over your vows, readings, and ceremony program or send these in an e-mail and call to discuss.

❑ **Touch-up**. Get your hair trimmed and roots dyed with your usual stylist.

❑ **Organize** your wedding day stuff.

    ❑ Assemble everything that will be on your body on the wedding day (from tiara to shoes and makeup to perfume), and put it all in one place. Suggestions for Dressing Room preparation items are on page 77.

    ❑ Gather everything that will be set up by a Helper at the ceremony and box it up with diagrams/instructions.

    ❑ Gather everything that will be set up by a Helper at the reception and box it up with diagrams/instructions.

❑ **Emergency kit** suggestions can also be found on page 77. Delegate this duty to a Helper or Wedding Coordinator.

❑ **Pack** for your wedding night and for your honeymoon, keeping in mind your airline's carry-on luggage rules. (Hint: pack one of everything in your carry-on luggage. If the checked baggage gets lost or delayed, you will at least have one complete outfit, a swim suit, and your toothbrush).

❑ **Photocopy** your marriage license and put the copy with your luggage. You can present it to the hotel as proof that you are on your honeymoon. Show it to every person who has the power to give you a freebie or an upgrade.

❑ **Toasts**. Write and practice any toasts that you and your Groom will be giving.

❑ **Pamper Yourself**. Get a massage. Practice some yoga. DO NOT try any new products or treatments on your face.

❑ **House Sitter**. Hire someone to take care of your pets, plants, and mail.

❑ **Engagement Ring**. Take your ring to the jeweler to get it cleaned and polished. Consider leaving your new jewelry behind when you go on the honeymoon, especially if it does not fit.

❑ **Credit Cards**. Inform your financial institutions of your travel plans. Strange charges on your credit card creates suspicion of theft and your bank could freeze them.

The Day Before

❑ **Set Up** the rehearsal venue with your décor, tables & chairs, photo booth, and specialty tables. Set up the wedding venue with your traditional fixtures, sign-in table, flowers, chairs, altar, backdrop, and décor.

❑ **Mani-Pedi**. Get your nails done. Treat your bridesmaids to the same. (Hint: make an appointment for after set-up).

❑ **Rehearse** the ceremony order of events with everyone involved: Bridal Party, VIPs, and Helpers. Let the wedding coordinator and the officiant run the show. Print out the order of events for the reception and talk through it with your Bridal Party and wedding coordinator.

❑ **Toast** your bridal party, VIP's, and Helpers at the rehearsal dinner, saying *thank you* to everyone who is participating in your big day. Show your gratitude by passing out gifts.

❑ **Go to bed** at a decent hour, even if you don't think you can sleep. The phrase "beauty rest" is no joke.

Wedding Day

- **Set up**. Some venues won't let you set up until the day of the wedding, and you are busy. In that case, let a Helper set up any décor or fixtures that you were unable to set up the day before.

- **Boarding Passes**. Print out your boarding passes 24 hours before your flight, and put them with your luggage. Give your itinerary and contact information to your parents or emergency contact.

- **Delegate**. Give the wedding rings and envelopes with your vendors' tips to the Maid of Honor or the Best Man.

- **Get Pretty**. Go to your hair & makeup appointments on time. Haul everything to the dressing room and stay there with the bridesmaids until go-time (Hint: have your photographer join you in the dressing room, catching candid moments). Pack up the dressing room before you leave for the ceremony. A Dressing Room Helper can take care of the bridal party's purses and the emergency kit, and make sure nothing is left behind in the dressing room.

- **Attire**. Confirm with a Helper where to meet you the day after the wedding. That person can take your wedding gown to a secure location and return the Groom's rented tuxedo/suit.

- **Follow** your wedding day schedule. Rely on your coordinator and wedding party to move the schedule along and to take care of any mishaps. If at the end of the day you are married, then it was a success!

- **Wedding Gifts**. Designate a Helper pack your gifts after the reception and transport them to a secure location.

- **Have Fun**. However, avoid getting drunk, especially if a videographer is present.

- **Leave**. Enjoy your honeymoon! Turn off your phone, and don't talk to anyone except your husband for at least a week. Your diet is over (or at least on hold), so savor anything you want. Trust your Helpers to follow through.

The Aftermath

- **Preserve**. Freeze the top layer (or a slice) of your wedding cake to eat on your first anniversary. Send your dress to be cleaned and/or preserved for future generations. Preserve your bouquet or some flower petals.

- **Announce**. Send your wedding announcement to the local newspaper or post pictures online.

- **Marriage License**. Send your completed marriage license to the proper authority. They will send it back to you.

- **Choose Photos**. Select the images from your photographer that you want to have framed or put in a photo album.

- **Change Your Name** (and your e-mail address, if it uses your old last name). Make a list of all your bills and every organization that sends you legitimate mail. Take a weekday off of work and take your marriage license to the Drivers License office, the Social Security office, and your bank. Go online or call the other organizations. (Hint: Plan any travel carefully during this time, so that the name on your plane ticket matches the name on your photo I.D.)

- **Give feedback**. Rate your vendors on wedding websites, to help future brides in their planning. If a vendor was really outstanding, send them a thank you note. Contact the author of *Bride on a Mission*, let her know what it was like to plan your wedding using this workbook, and offer your feedback.

- **Say Thanks**. Start writing thank you notes for wedding gifts as soon as possible - like on the plane ride home from your honeymoon. (Hint: You technically have one year, but after two months someone will ask you if your monogrammed salad spinner got lost in the mail).

- **Mentally prepare** for everyone's next question, "So... when are you going to have a baby?" It will happen. Soon.

The Budget

The question that got this all started was "Will you marry me?" Since you said *yes*, the next question should be, "How do you want to marry me?" Before you go shopping for reception tablecloths, it is important to get on the same page with your fiancé. Typically, when most grooms propose, they have no idea what they are getting themselves into. Since most brides have never participated in planning a wedding before, you and your fiancé need to discuss your expectations. How do you expect to make this wedding happen? The decision that has the biggest impact on your wedding day is the least romantic and the most delicate: the budget.

You and your fiancé have three budgetary topics to discuss and attempt to agree upon: (1) How much you should budget to spend on your wedding, (2) where all that dough will be coming from, and then (3) how, where, and when to spend it.

Getting married costs a minimum of $50... legally, but that only covers the marriage license. *Having a wedding*, on the other hand, can easily cost in the tens of thousands of dollars. It all depends on the choices that you make right now. All that dough has to come from somewhere. A wedding is not a good reason to go into debt.

Your family may give you money for your wedding as a gift, but some may feel entitled to make decisions about what they are paying for. Find out what strings are attached before you deposit a big check from your parents (or other sponsor). Ask the following question: "When you say you want to help with the wedding, what do you envision?" Answers may vary from "Going wedding dress shopping with you" to "Choosing your band's music for you so that I can be sure they don't embarrass me." There is more about this on page 87.

There is more about this on page 87.

Ideas to slim-down a Wedding Budget

for the Crafty Bride:
find tutorials on your wedding crafts. List any crafting tools that you will need but don't have. Borrow what you can from your fellow crafters.

for the Thrifty Bride:
Start your shopping online. Look for lovingly made but gently used wedding items.

for the Feisty Bride:
ask your like-minded guests to sponsor one of your wedding expenses. Instead of getting place settings, ask for something that you need now, like a keg of beer for the reception.

The Shopping List (how it works and how to use it)

The Checklist (page 3) and The Shopping List (page 12) are two sides of the same coin. To put on a wedding and reception, there is a long list of items and services that you will need to buy, rent, borrow, or hire. The Shopping List is an attempt to gather and organize all such wedding paraphernalia. This list includes columns to help you track the costs. First, decide which items on the list to boot off, thus making room for what matters to you. Then chip away at the list until it is all done or the money runs out.

BUDGET SERVING SUGGESTIONS

To get started organizing your expenses, slice up your budget by category, starting with these suggested percentages. Fill in the dollar amounts in *The Shopping List* on the following page.

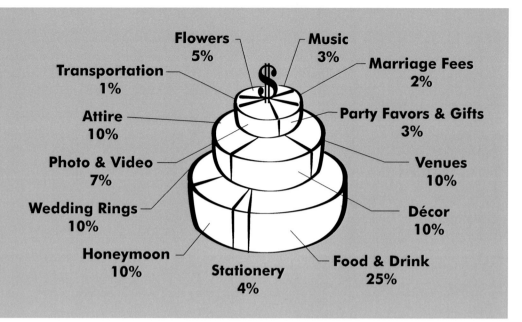

Flowers 5%
Music 3%
Transportation 1%
Marriage Fees 2%
Attire 10%
Party Favors & Gifts 3%
Photo & Video 7%
Venues 10%
Wedding Rings 10%
Décor 10%
Honeymoon 10%
Food & Drink 25%
Stationery 4%

Worksheet: Contributors to the Budget

	Dollar Amount	Percentage	Specific Expenses
Bride			
Bride's Mother			
Bride's Father			
Bride's Grandparents			
Bride's Grandparents			
Bride's _____			
Groom			
Groom's Mother			
Groom's Father			
Groom's Grandparents			
Groom's Grandparents			
Groom's _____			
TOTAL		NOTES	

11

The Shopping List

STATIONERY 4% = _____	TARGET BUDGET	ADJUSTED BUDGET	VENDOR/PROVIDER	PAYMENT DUE DATE
Notebook & bridal magazines				
Engagement announcement				
Save-The-Dates				
Invitation package				
Envelopes/pochettes				
Envelope seals/stickers				
Calligrapher/printable labels				
Rehearsal Dinner invitations				
Stamps				
Programs				
Sign-in book & pen				
Pew cards/reserved seating signs				
Menus				
Table numbers & seat assignments				
Reception signage				
Thank you cards				
New address announcements				

VENUES 10% = _____				
Church/ceremony venue rental fee				
Reception venue rental fee				
Trash services & portable toilets				
Support staff (see page 31)				

MARRIAGE FEES 2% = _____				
Officiant fee				
Marriage preparation program				
Marriage license				
Wedding consultant/coordinator				

WEDDING RINGS 10% = _____	TARGET BUDGET	ADJUSTED BUDGET	VENDOR/PROVIDER	PAYMENT DUE DATE
Bride's wedding band				
Groom's wedding band				
Engraving				
Insurance				
Resizing program				

ATTIRE 10% = _____				
Bride's wedding gown + alterations				
Bride's jewelry				
Bride's hairpiece/veil				
Bride's foundation garments				
Garter				
Bride's shoes				
Bride's purse				
Bride's hairstyle & makeup				
Groom's tux or suit				
Groom's accessories				
Bridesmaids' accent piece				
Bridesmaids' hairstyles & makeup				
Flower girl's basket				
Ring bearer's pillow				
Wedding gown preservation				

MUSIC 3% = _____				
Ceremony musicians/cantor				
Reception DJ or band				
Equipment rental				

TRANSPORTATION 1% = _____				
Bride & Groom's wedding day ride				
Guest busses, shuttles, or parking				

13

continued →

		TARGET BUDGET	ADJUSTED BUDGET	VENDOR/PROVIDER	PAYMENT DUE DATE
FLOWERS	5% = _____				
Bride's bouquet & toss bouquet					
Boutonnieres					
Bridesmaids' bouquets					
Flower girl's bouquet/petals					
Floral hairpieces					
Corsages					
Flowers for the décor					
DÉCOR	10% = _____				
Traditional fixtures for ceremony					
Chairs & aisle decorations for ceremony					
Tables & chairs for reception					
Linens (table cloths, runners, napkins)					
Lighting					
Centerpieces					
Box/birdcage for envelopes					
Specialty tables & their decorations					
HONEYMOON	10% = _____				
Passports					
Travelers Cheques					
Accommodations on wedding night					
Airfare & airport parking					
Honeymoon lodging					
Honeymoon car rental/taxi fare					
Food & drink					
Cash for tips					
Excursions & souvenirs					
Vaccines (for international travel)					

FOOD & DRINK 25% = _____	TARGET BUDGET	ADJUSTED BUDGET	VENDOR/PROVIDER	PAYMENT DUE DATE
Rehearsal dinner catering/restaurant				
Reception appetizers				
Reception catering, fees, & tips				
Wedding cake & topper				
Groom's cake				
Other desserts				
Cake stands				
Beer, wine, alcohol, mixers, & soft drinks				
Bartender fee & tip				
Personalized items (i.e. cocktail napkins)				
Cake knife & spatula				
Toasting chalices				
Place settings & glassware				

PARTY FAVORS & GIFTS 3% = _____				
Bridesmaids' gifts				
Groomsmen gifts				
Flower girl and ring bearer gifts				
Gifts for moms & dads				
Grand exit (bubbles, sparklers, etc.)				
Party favors for guests				

PHOTO & VIDEO 7% = _____				
Engagement portraits				
Bridal portraits				
Slideshow for rehearsal or reception				
Wedding day photographer & tip				
Photo booth or backdrop at reception				
Photo albums for couple & parents				
Videographer fee & tip				
Extra copies of wedding video				

continued →

OTHER (you decide)	TARGET BUDGET	ADJUSTED BUDGET	VENDOR/PROVIDER	PAYMENT DUE DATE

VENDOR/PROVIDER	CONTACT INFORMATION	NOTES

Guests

The Bridal Party

BRIDAL PARTY (NOUN): the folks who stand with the Bride & Groom at the Ceremony. This group is includes the Best Man, Maid/Matron of Honor, the Groomsmen, the Bridesmaids, the Ring Bearer, and the Flower Girl. A.K.A. The Attendants or The Wedding Party.

On your wedding day, you will want to be surrounded with the people who love you the most, and who can tolerate you when you are stressed. When you ask these people to be your Attendants, they become your first invited guests.

The size of your Bridal Party matters. For a list of attendants' jobs, see page 82. If you have too few attendants, it puts a lot of responsibility on just a few shoulders. With too many attendants, it can be difficult to coordinate every last person's calendar for all of the pre-wedding events.

Remember that these folks have the right to say *no* and for any reason. Being in a Bridal Party can be expensive (financially as well as emotionally), between the attire, travel, and all the parties. If someone shocks you by saying *no*, offer to help with the cost. Still *no*? Move on to another candidate. As for the flower girl and ring bearer, their parents may say *no* for reasons that don't make sense to you, and that is very common. Ask someone else, but still invite them to attend.

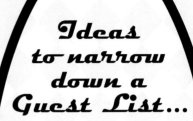

Ideas to narrow down a Guest List...

For the Crafty Bride
Send your Save-The-Date to some, but not all of the invitees. The Save-The-Dates are hand made and very time consuming, after all. Those invitees left out may make other plans before they receive their invitation.

For the Thrifty Bride
If your parents insist on inviting people outside of your Circle of Invitees, then ask them to cover the per-head cost for their extra guests.

For the Feisty Bride
Have a destination wedding (see page 88).

17

continued →

The Guest List

Whom should you invite? Not only the size, but the style and cost of your wedding may greatly depend upon the answer. Triple digits of guests means that your reception will be loud, and you can't use a quaint bed and breakfast as a venue. On the plus side, if your venue is already huge, it's no problem to add another twenty guests. With a small guest list, the venue should be proportionate. A cathedral, for example, would feel cavernous with a small group, but a gazebo would feel intimate.

Some couples want their wedding reception to be an adult-only soirée. If you exclude children, know that some parents will feel excluded as well. Some people jump at the chance to go to a wedding kid-free, but not every parent does.

As you think of more and more people you'd like to invite, their relationship to you gets more and more obscure. Decide with your fiancé where to draw the line, which is more like a circle around the two of you. The bigger you draw the circle, the more invitees fit within it. When you select your Circle of Invitees, ask yourselves the following:

- Is 50% of guests for the Bride and 50% for the Groom a reasonable division, considering the size of your families?

- If you draw the Circle of Invitees too small, will there be people genuinely hurt by the exclusion?

- You talk to the butcher more than your childhood best friend, but who do you want to dance with at the reception?

- There may be people outside the Circle of Invitees who are still very dear to one of you, how may exceptions are okay?

Table Number	Outer Envelope Name	Address		
		Line 1	Line 2	Line 3
1	The Jefferson Family	100 First Street	New Dallas, TX 77777	
	Miss Roosevelt	200 Second Street	Apartment 300	New Dallas, TX 77777
2	Dr. & Mrs. Franklin	300 Third Street	New Dallas, TX 77777	
4	The Adams Family	400 Fourth Street	New Dallas, TX 77777	

EXAMPLE: GUEST ADDRESS SPREADSHEET

Select your Circle of Invitees

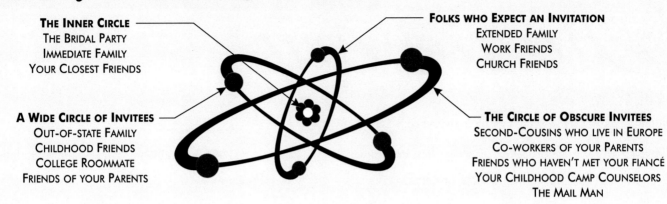

THE INNER CIRCLE
THE BRIDAL PARTY
IMMEDIATE FAMILY
YOUR CLOSEST FRIENDS

FOLKS WHO EXPECT AN INVITATION
EXTENDED FAMILY
WORK FRIENDS
CHURCH FRIENDS

A WIDE CIRCLE OF INVITEES
OUT-OF-STATE FAMILY
CHILDHOOD FRIENDS
COLLEGE ROOMMATE
FRIENDS OF YOUR PARENTS

THE CIRCLE OF OBSCURE INVITEES
SECOND-COUSINS WHO LIVE IN EUROPE
CO-WORKERS OF YOUR PARENTS
FRIENDS WHO HAVEN'T MET YOUR FIANCÉ
YOUR CHILDHOOD CAMP COUNSELORS
THE MAIL MAN

Spreadsheet

As you start your guest list, save your sanity and create a spreadsheet. With a digital spreadsheet, the data can translate into address labels. The columns can go on forever, but start with Name, Address, and Response. If your guests have a meal option in the RSVP, then add a column for those responses. The column for "Baby" is a way to count each little guest who will need a seat at the reception but will not need a meal. Columns for table numbers, gifts received, and thank you notes are an added bonus.

Collecting addresses is big job, so get help. Someone in your family is bound to have mailed graduation or baby announcements recently, so ask for their address book as a starting point. Then get your parents' and grandparents' address books. As a last resort, call or send an e-mail to invitees, asking for their current address. If you send out a mass e-mail, use the BCC line to protect everyone's privacy.

Inner Envelope Name	Number of Invitees	RSVP YES			RSVP NO	Rehearsal Dinner RSVP	Gift	Thank You Note
		Meal 1	Meal 2	Baby				
Frank, Hazel, Jenna & Guest	5	3	2			5		
Julie & Guest	2				2		Plates	✓
Grandpa & Grandma	2	2						
James, Jamie, and James Junior	3	2		1			Candles	

EXAMPLE: TRACKING RESPONSES + BONUS COLUMNS

Stationery

Stationary (ADJECTIVE): standing still; not moving.

Stationery (NOUN): all the paper products that are printed or crafted for a wedding & reception. Some examples include:

- Engagement Announcements/Party Invitations
- Wedding Invitation Package
- Wedding Programs
- Reception Menu Cards
- New Address Announcements

- Save-The-Dates
- Guest Sign-In Book
- Reception Table Assignments & Name Cards
- Reception Signage
- Thank You Notes

Invitation Discussion Topics:

Paper: color, handmade, cotton, textured, recycled, vellum, scoring (for folding)

Textured Text: thermography, letterpress, engraving

Flat Text: calligraphy, digital printing, offset printing, rubber stamp

Envelopes: outer/inner, color, liner pattern/color, pochette, square, shaped flap

Embellishments: ribbon, rubber stamp, dried flowers, address labels, seals, crafty bits

Extra Fees: rush order, shipping, assembly, additional orders, return address

Others: sample vs. proof, turn-around time, deposit required

Typical Invitation Package:

Wedding Invitation Card - can be done in all kinds of different ways, and it establishes the theme for the rest of your stationery. May require tissue paper to keep ink from sticking to the other items.

RSVP Card - where guests check yes or no, veal or vegetarian, and any other census information that you need.

Stamped Envelope - addressed to the person collecting the RSVPs.

Accommodation Card - so your out-of-town guests know where they'll get a group rate.

Rehearsal Dinner Invitation - for the Bridal Party, VIPs, and out-of-town guests. Include directions/map. (Hint: This event can turn into a big party all on its own.)

Reception Card - this contains the address of the reception venue and any other important information. If your reception venue is within walking distance of the wedding venue, then skip this. One day, everyone will have a GPS, but that day is not yet here, so print a large map on the back of the card.

Inner Envelope - specify who is invited and if a "plus one" is welcome. If you skip the inner envelope, then there is no place to specify who is invited. In that case, phrases like "adults only" or "no pets, please" can go on the reception card.

Outer Envelope - formally addressed to the recipient's household and its is loaded with etiquette. Search the internet for the best wording for each particular situation. The return address belongs to the Bride or to the host. Heads up: if the envelope is square or heavy, it will require extra postage.

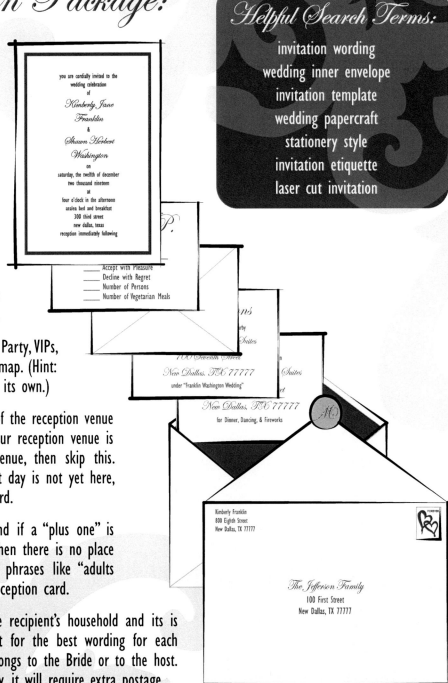

21

continued →

Wedding Invitation Text Samples

Example A:
Both Parents are Hosting
Catholic Ceremony
Lots of Capitalization

Example B:
Bride's Parents are Hosting
Protestant Ceremony

Example C:
Couple is Hosting
Civil Ceremony
No Capitalization

Kimberly Jane

Franklin

and

Shawn Herbert

Washington

Together with their Parents
Request the Honor of your Presence
at their Nuptial Mass
to be Celebrated on
Saturday, the Twelfth of December
Two Thousand Nineteen
at
Four o'clock in the Afternoon
St. Paul Catholic Church
100 First Street
New Dallas, Texas
Reception to Follow

Benjamin & Aretha Franklin
request your attendance
at the marriage ceremony
joining their daughter

Kimberly Jane

to

Shawn Herbert

Washington

son of
George & Carrie Washington
on
Saturday, the Twelfth of December
two thousand nineteen
at
four o'clock in the afternoon
Fourteenth Baptist Church
200 Second Street
New Dallas, Texas
reception immediately following

---

you are cordially invited to the
wedding celebration
of

Kimberly Jane

Franklin

&

Shawn Herbert

Washington

on
saturday, the twelfth of december
two thousand nineteen
at
four o'clock in the afternoon
azalea bed and breakfast
300 third street
new dallas, texas
reception immediately following

22

Invitation Presentation Ideas

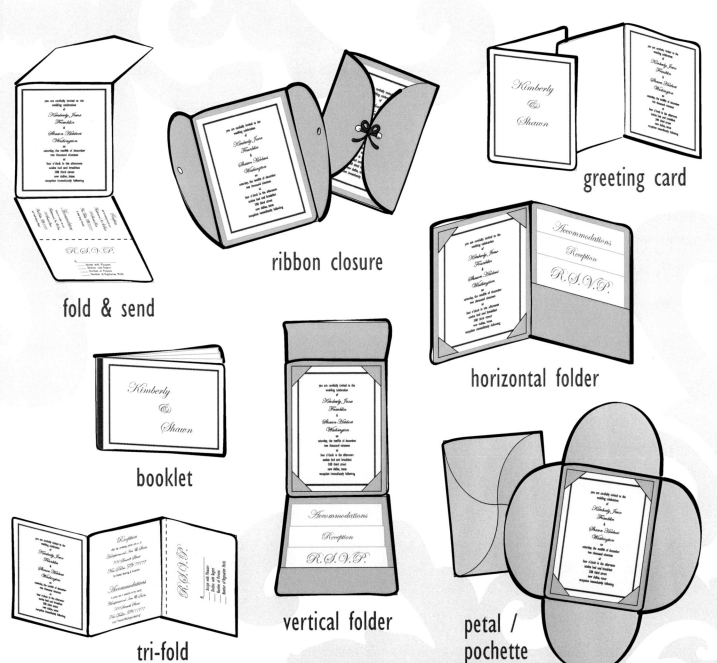

fold & send

ribbon closure

greeting card

booklet

horizontal folder

tri-fold

vertical folder

petal / pochette

23

continued →

Ways to Make Invitations:

Method Desription	Crafty Scale	Thrifty Scale	Feisty Scale
Print invitations at home on vellum, dress them up with crafty bits or fancy inner envelopes.	✂✂✂✂✂	$ $ $	👄 👄
Design your invitation on a computer as a JPG file and order photographs of the image.	✂✂✂✂	$	👄 👄 👄
Order simple thermography ink invitations and embellish with a rubber stamp or water color.	✂✂✂	$ $ $ $	👄 👄 👄
Buy a do-it-yourself kit, design the text on a computer, and print at home.	✂✂	$ $ $	👄 👄
Choose a design and order your invitations through an online invitation vendor.	✂	$ $	👄 👄 👄
Visit a wedding store or print shop and choose from their selection of invitations.	✂	$ $ $ $ $	👄 👄 👄 👄
Order rubber stamps with the invitation text and design elements, stamp your own paper.	✂✂✂	$ $ $	👄 👄 👄
Order your invitations from a crafty person.	✂✂✂✂	$ $ $ $	👄 👄 👄 👄
Get one invitation made, take a fun photo of it, and order photographs of the image.	✂✂	$ $	👄 👄 👄

Key to Symbols:

✂✂✂ More Crafty	$ $ $ More Expensive	👄 👄 👄 These don't
✂ Less Crafty	$ Less Expensive	👄 mean anything

Ideas to Simplify an Invitation Package

For the Crafty Bride:
design the RSVP card as a postcard, which eliminates the need for an envelope & it requires less postage.

For the Thrifty Bride:
combine the Map/Reception card with the Accommodation card. Print on the front and the back.

For the Feisty Bride:
for your guests who were born after 1980, skip the mailed RSVP protocol. On your RSVP card, put your e-mail address or a link to your wedding website's response page.

Programs keep your guests informed and entertained before and during the Wedding Ceremony

Possible Contents of a Ceremony Program:
- Time, Date, and Location of Ceremony
- Your new Monogram or Design Elements from your Invitations
- Names of Bridal Party and Procession (you may include their relationship to the bride and groom)
- Officiant Name & Title (and how you know him/her)
- Order of Events in the Ceremony
- Song Titles & Artists from the Ceremony
- Readings from the Ceremony (either the source of the reading or the long form so guests can read along)
- Special Thanks
- In Memoriam
- Special Message/Sentiment addresses to your Guests
- Reception Schedule
- Map & Directions to the Reception

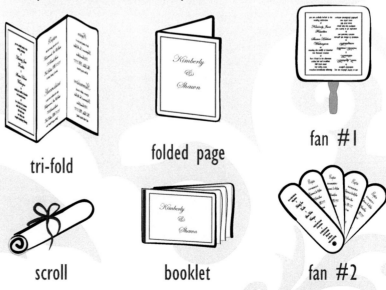

tri-fold

folded page

fan #1

scroll

booklet

fan #2

continued →

Reception Stationery can inform and organize your guests at the reception.

Table Assignments, Name/Place/Escort Cards, Table Numbers, and "Reserved" Signs - if you serve dinner, these items help your guests to find their seats in an orderly fashion. The upside to these items: they are a huge opportunity for crafting, you get to be in control of the seating arrangements (either to encourage new people to meet or old foes to stay separate), you don't need extra seating. The downside: it's a lot of organizing, you have to wait for the final headcount, and then the tables are a lot of work to set up.

Menu Cards - describe the food available, but you don't need to have waiters to justify Menu Cards. They are especially helpful if there are lots of choices, several courses, or there is a backstory to the food selections.

Reception Signage - keeps your guests from getting lost, directs them to the restrooms, and makes sure everyone knows about the fun things that are planned. Signage may include:

- Arrows directing cars to "turn here" or "more parking ahead"
- Explanation of each Specialty Table/Area, such as "How to Use the Photo Booth"
- Special Instructions, such as, "Please Help Yourself to Appetizers" or "Do Not Feed the Bears"
- Special Announcements, such as, "Please Stay for Fireworks after Sunset"

Signage Display Ideas

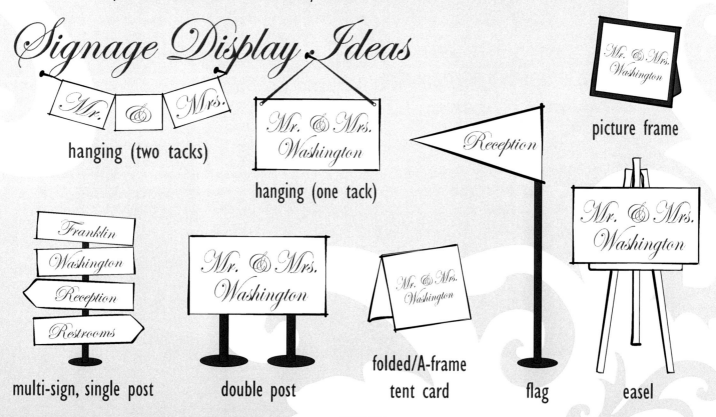

hanging (two tacks)

hanging (one tack)

picture frame

multi-sign, single post

double post

folded/A-frame
tent card

flag

easel

Place Card Presentation Ideas for an apple theme.

Place cards go hand-in-hand with table assignments and table numbers at the reception. If you do not assign seating, you will need to have extra chairs available - to fill in for odd numbers and people's natural tendency to leave an empty chair between themselves and someone they do not know.

folded paper with apple logo

apple-shaped paper

actual apple with paper tag

Ideas for Signing-In Without a Book

For the Crafty Bride: make a "tree" out of bare branches, a vase, and leaf-shaped paper tags. Your guests can sign the tags and hang them from the tree.

For the Thrifty Bride: provide an uncommon object and permanent markers (which come in black, metallic, and a slew of colors). Ask your guests for their autographs.

For the Feisty Bride: use a photo of you and your Groom. Choose a frame with a large white mat, leave out the glass, and invite guests to sign the mat.

Venues

A wedding and reception can occur in all kinds of spaces. The venues could be outside or indoors, within walking distance or remote, and full-service or Spartan. Rearrange the chairs after the ceremony, and the wedding venue can morph into the reception venue. With any space, some things must exist: a place to stand/sit/dance, room to move around, room to put food/drink/gifts, and access to a restroom.

Venues range from a blank canvas to a one-stop shop. If you are getting married under water, you must provide every last thing - right down to the oxygen. If you go through a wedding drive-thru, you just have to show up. The cost to use a venue will depend on it's facilities, services, regulating body, location, and popularity.

Before you choose your venue(s), talk to the people in charge - not just about available dates - but about your vision and about their fees and rules. A park ranger could veto the use of fireworks. The secretary at a church may tell you that strapless dresses are not allowed. If a winery has a policy to discourage outside suppliers, the uncorking fees can add up fast.

Make appointments to tour the venues that meet your criteria and availability. Take note of the fixtures and colors in those spaces, so you can coordinate with them or make plans to cover them up. Find rental facilities or vendors to fill the gaps in the items and services that you will need.

Venue Ideas...

for the Crafty Bride: start from scratch with a barn, a beach, or a backyard. With that comes full creative control, including how to decorate the portable toilets that must be rented.

for the Thrifty Bride: rent out a Bed & Breakfast and use it for all of your events: the rehearsal dinner, wedding ceremony, reception, wedding night, and brunch the following day.

for the Feisty Bride: go for a full service venue like a hotel or a wedding chapel. If you prefer an offbeat venue, an art gallery or a dinner cruise would have staff accustomed to hosting a party.

Ceremony Seating

Guest Seating
Altar/Stage
Aisle

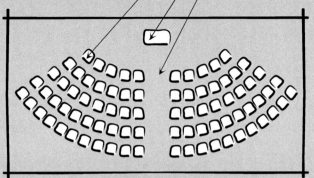

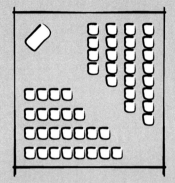

Traditional Seating
7~10 sq. ft. per guest
+ aisle and altar.
Simple to set up.

Curved or Circular Seating
10~12 sq. ft. per guest
+ aisle and altar. Good
for large or open spaces.

Angled Seating Plan
7~10 sq. ft. per guest
+ aisle and altar.
Good for square spaces.

Table Space Requirements

Minimum distance between tables: 5 feet. Allow space for walkways.

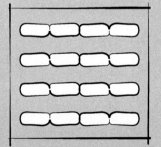

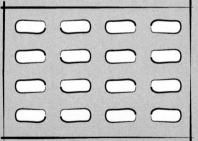

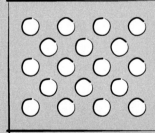

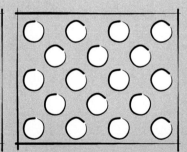

End-to-end banquet style tables: 8 sq. ft. per guest.

8' banquet tables: 10 sq. ft. per guest (seat 8 to 10 guests per table).

60" round tables: 10 to 12 sq. ft. per guest (seat up to 10 per table).

72" round tables: 12 to 14 sq. ft. per guest (seat up to 12 per table).

Reception Venue Space

DANCE FLOOR	
	GUEST TABLES
BUFFET & SPECIALTY TABLES	

Dance Floor in the Center

	BUFFET
DANCE FLOOR	**GUEST TABLES**
	SPECIALTY TABLES

Dance Floor at the Helm

- Plan for the dance floor space to hold 9 square feet per dancing couple plus a stage, a bandstand, or a DJ's table and equipment.

- The buffet may display the hors d'oeuvres, dinner, dessert, drinks, or all four.

- Specialty tables should be separate from the seating area and visible from the entrance or along a common path, in order to attract your guests' attention. A common path might be the way to the restroom or the way to the open bar. Otherwise, your guests may not know where to sign in, where to leave a gift, or that they can visit a photo booth to make a souvenir.

- For a cocktail reception (with few or no tables), budget for 10 square feet per guest plus dance floor.

Venue Notes _____

_____
_____
_____
_____
_____
_____

Venue Discussion Topics:

Space:
square footage _____
maximum capacity _____
bridal party dressing rooms _____
tents _____
dance floor _____
wheelchair accessibility _____
area for smoking _____
parking spaces _____

Restrooms:
capacity _____
supply of toilet paper _____
supply of paper towels _____
baby changing station _____

Facilities:
trash disposal _____
lighting _____
sound system _____
kitchen _____
ice maker _____
power sources _____
climate control _____
    fans _____
    air conditioning _____
    fireplaces _____
    portable heaters _____
fire extinguishers _____
permits required _____
liquor license _____
emergency exits _____

Tables:
number of tables & chairs _____
linens _____
table settings _____
serving ware _____
serving dishes _____
bar and bar ware _____

Support Staff:
setup & takedown _____
catering _____
bartending _____
preferred DJ or band _____
wait staff _____
busboys _____
restroom attendant _____
coat room attendant _____
security guard _____

Décor:
what fixtures in the space are permanent/
    which are movable? _____
what décor is available? _____
are thumbtacks & tape allowed? _____
are candls allowed? _____
preferred supplier _____

Costs and Terms:
taxes, fees, & payment terms _____
contract terms & conditions _____
fee for extra hours _____
when do the doors open for set-up and
    ceremony/reception? _____

Note: every venue has different resources available, use this list to find the right fit for you.

Ceremony Venue Sketch

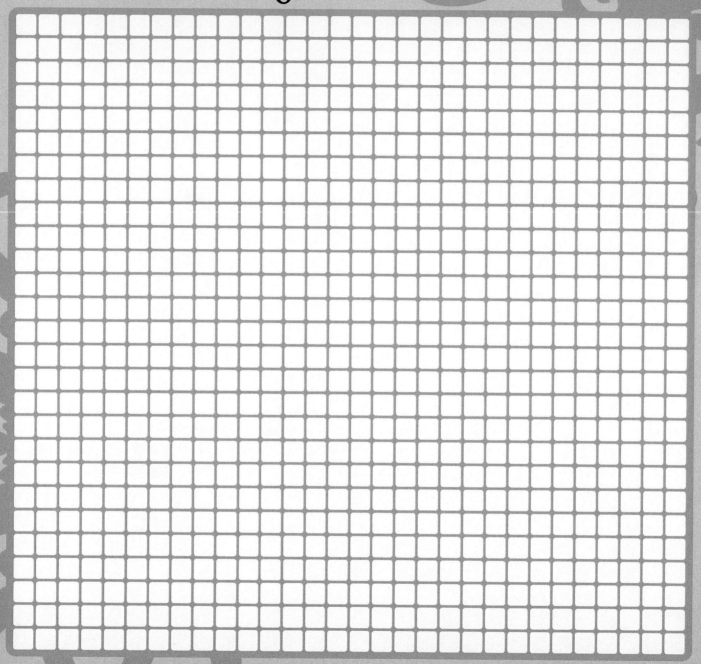

Reception Venue Sketch

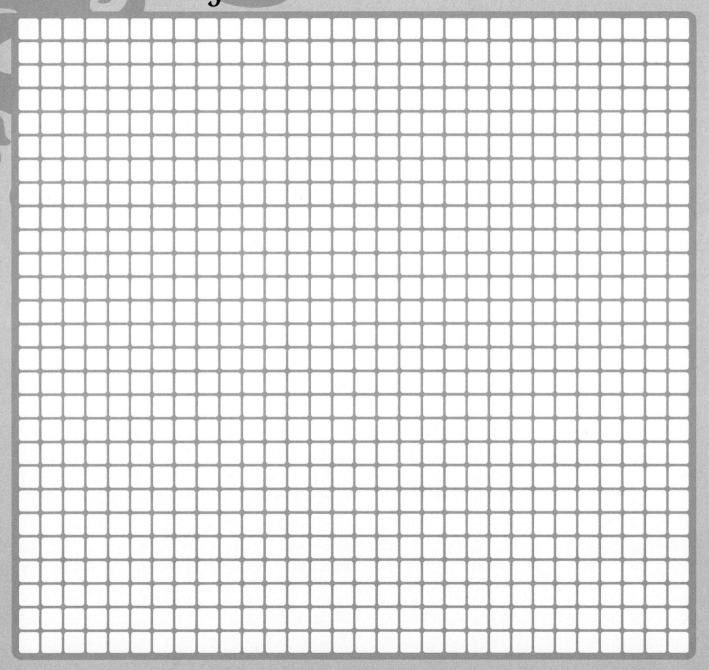

décor set the stage & showcase your style

The term *décor* can encompass a great many things. It is everything bought, rented, or borrowed for a wedding that you neither wear nor eat. The ceremony décor includes the backdrop, seating, and aisle. The reception décor (literally) covers the tables, chairs, walls, floor, and ceiling. Select your décor with your theme and color scheme in mind. Complement each focal point with its background. But always remember, when the wedding is over with, all this décor has to go somewhere (like in an attic or to a charity).

ceremony backdrop ideas

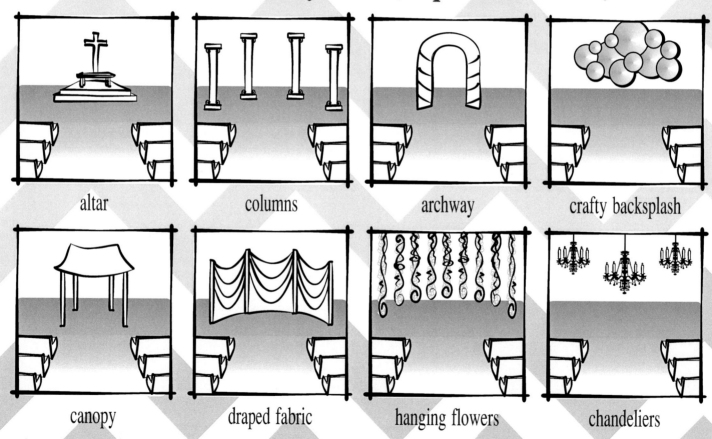

altar

columns

archway

crafty backsplash

canopy

draped fabric

hanging flowers

chandeliers

a truly personal décor scheme...

for the Crafty Bride: provide containers to your florist that you have sculpted, painted, or bedazzled to make them personal.

for the Thrifty Bride: decorate your wedding with objects, fabrics, and candles that can later decorate your home. You can put items on your registry for this very purpose.

for the Feisty Bride: choose a reception venue that is so beautiful that decorations are unnecessary. Place appetizers on the tables instead of centerpieces.

aisle decoration ideas

Inside or outdoors, the aisle completes the wedding scene.

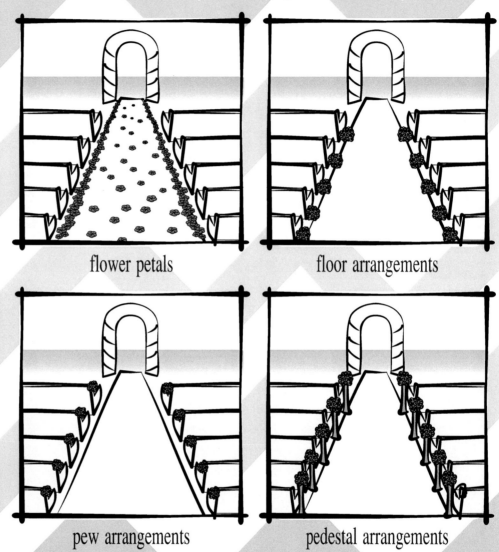

flower petals

floor arrangements

pew arrangements

pedestal arrangements

Aisle Runner (noun): a fabric or paper roll of material that runs the length of the aisle. It is unrolled by a Helper prior to the Bride's entrance. Known to catch on high heels and cause stumbling.

centerpieces

As a major focal point of the reception, the table decor gets a lot of attention. Imagine the entire room when you choose the centerpieces. Keep in mind your guests and how they will interact with the items there.

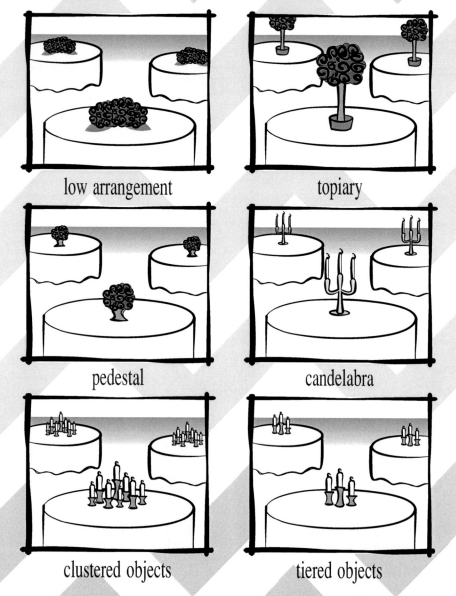

low arrangement

topiary

pedestal

candelabra

clustered objects

tiered objects

centerpiece building materials

antiques
balloons
birdcages
board games
books
bowls
buckets
candles (wax or LED)
cornucopia
cowboy boots
crystal
feathers
flowers/leaves/twigs
food/drinks
fruit
glassware
goldfish (living)
lamps/lanterns
mirrors
party favors
paper/crafts
photos
potted plants
pumpkins
ribbon
rocks (aquarium or river)
seashells
water (clear or dyed)
wine bottles

design considerations when selecting materials

- colors – how many colors and how those colors interact. The spray paint aisle & the paint chip section of the hardware store and the fabric section of the craft store are a good place to start. Compart bold contrast to subtle shades and find the right fit.
- contrast of foreground to background(s) – i.e. the centerpiece against the table and then the table against the wall or the bouquets against the bridesmaid dresses.
- light transmission (examples)
  opaque – heavy fabric & solid objects
  translucent – sheer fabric, lace, & frosted glass
  transparent – glass, crystal, & water
  reflective – glitter, shiny fabric, and mirror
  patterns (mix of patterns and solids)
- repetition vs. variety
- texture – create layers of texture as well as color

helpful search terms

reception layout
wedding color scheme
centerpiece hack
paper flower tutorial
easy seating chart
hot glue wedding

color combination ideas

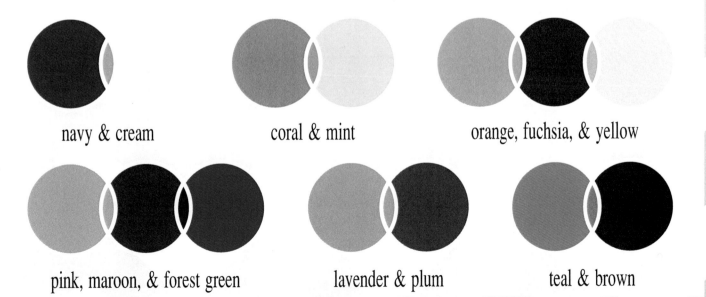

navy & cream

coral & mint

orange, fuchsia, & yellow

pink, maroon, & forest green

lavender & plum

teal & brown

table setting options

A formal place setting varies with the menu selection and the atmosphere of the reception. You may load the tables with stuff or leave implements where the guests can find them.

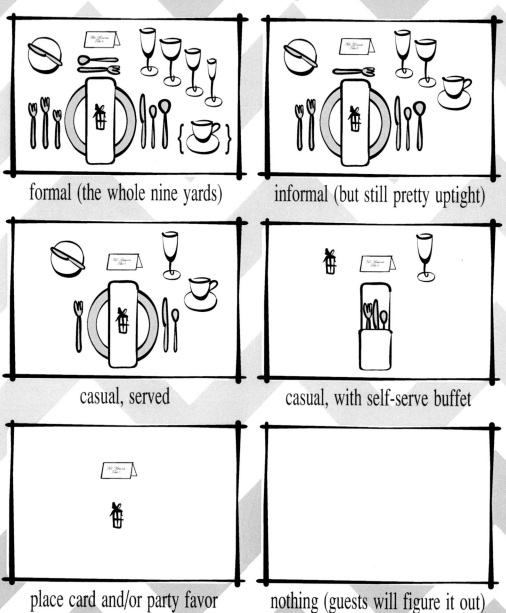

formal (the whole nine yards)

informal (but still pretty uptight)

casual, served

casual, with self-serve buffet

place card and/or party favor

nothing (guests will figure it out)

decoration idea sketches

Flowers... fresh-cut, artificial, or handcrafted.

Where to Use Flowers

Ceremony:
- Aisle decorations
- Altar/podium
- Traditional fixtures

Bridal Party:
- Bouquets
- Corsages
- Boutonnieres
- Hair pieces
- Toss bouquet

Reception:
- Centerpieces
- Doorways, columns
- Toss petals

Other:
- Bride & groom's car
- Cake topper
- Photo op spot

Flower Arrangement Ideas

...for the Thrifty Bride
- Incorporate less expensive flowers like baby's breath or white carnations.
- Grow your own flowers or pick wild flowers.
- Use your bridal party's bouquets as centerpieces at the reception.
- Carry a bouquet alternative that can be reused, like a purse, fan, book, lantern, Bible, candle, or parasol.

...for the Crafty Bride
- Incorporate inanimate objects into your bouquet, like buttons, feathers, LED candles, origami, glass ornaments, photographs, or even candy!
- Carry your flowers in an unusual vessel, like in a purse, galvanized bucket, or other item that you can decorate yourself.
- Order hearty flowers from a wholesaler and make your floral pieces totally custom.

...for the Feisty Bride
- Make a toss bouquet out of something that the single ladies will want to fight for - like gift cards, candy, or lottery tickets.
- After the wedding, donate your arrangements to a local hospital or nursing home.

Bouquet Shapes... stems may be hand-tied or uniform length.

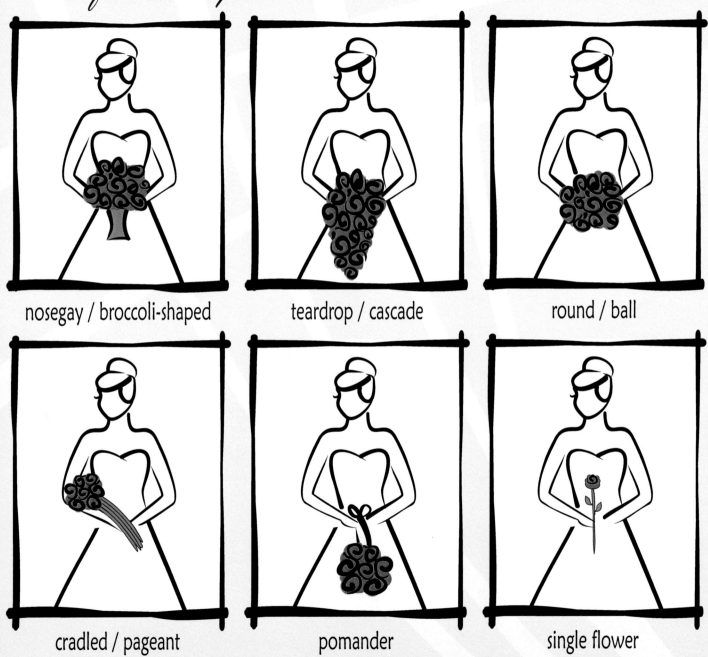

nosegay / broccoli-shaped

teardrop / cascade

round / ball

cradled / pageant

pomander

single flower

Bouquet & Arrangement Schemes

single species of
small flower

single species of
medium flower

single species of
large flower

single species of
jumbo flower

different colors,
single size of flower

same color, mix of
flower sizes

mix of sizes and
colors of flower

succulents - can
be replanted

Helpful Floral Search Terms

single bloom
hand tied bouquet
flower seasons
cascading centerpiece

paper bouquet
centerpiece alternative
toss bouquet
flower girl ideas

Bouquet Considerations

- As you design the size of your bouquet, consider how heavy it will be and how much of the gown it will hide.
- Use a minimum of flowers that have a strong scent. Your wedding party and guests may have severe allergies.
- Hold your bouquet at your navel, not at your cleavage (like you're scared), or at your side (like you don't care).

Florist Discussion Topics

Bring with you:
- Your likes, dislikes, and general vision for the bouquets & décor flowers
- Description, colors, and photos of the ceremony and reception venues
- Flower Distribution List (who gets a corsage, boutonniere, or bouquet)

Ask for:
- Examples of past work & contact information for past customers
- What flowers are in-season at the time of the wedding and the cost of any out-of-season demands
- A site visit to plan the scope of the Florist Contract, if décor is involved
- Instructions for keeping blooms fresh throughout the day's events
- Vessels and other inanimate objects available for rent
- Cost & turnaround time of a sample centerpiece and sample bouquet
- Deadline for final quantity updates
- Fees for delivery/set-up/breakdown
- Contract terms & conditions, payment schedule

Arrangement Vessels

The focal point of the centerpiece can be the vessel,
the flower arrangement, or both.

Urn   Basket   Glass Vase   Pot   Topiary

Notes from Florist Meeting

_____

_____

_____

_____

_____

_____

_____

_____

_____

_____

Bouquet Idea Sketches

attire

Brace yourself. The opinions are coming. But the most important opinion is your own. When you see your gown in the mirror, you should feel something. That's how you know that a dress is right for you. However, before you buy something you can't return, give yourself some time to think on it.

Obviously, keep the budget in mind. Maybe not so obvious: the weather, the setting, and the long-term plans. A light sheath will leave you freezing in the fall, and a heavy ball gown on the beach will make you sweat off your makeup. Stiletto heels do not mix with nature, especially sand. A house of worship may require dresses to have straps or even sleeves. At some point, ask yourself: *what is to become of this gown once the wedding is over?* Will your bridesmaids *really* wear their dresses again?

IDEAS FOR WEDDING GOWN SHORTCUTS

FOR THE CRAFTY BRIDE:

Look for a used gown in thrift & consignment stores. Buy one with a timeless bodice and skirt. Remove the eighties-tastic sleeves. Build your dream dress with the hard parts already done.

FOR THE THRIFTY BRIDE:

Many wedding dress retailers sell bridesmaid dresses in any color, including white and ivory. The downside: no train or bustle.

FOR THE FEISTY BRIDE:

Rent it! There are designer dresses for rent at a fraction of the cost of buying a gown new. You will not even have to dry clean it after the wedding.

PARTS OF THE BRIDAL ENSEMBLE

headpiece (i.e. tiara)

veil

sleeves

neckline

bodice (top half)

waist

bustle (where train is gathered for the reception)

skirt (bottom half)

silhouette (overall shape of the gown)

train (drags on the floor)

WEDDING GOWN SOUL SEARCHING:

BEFORE YOU SHOP

I want to wear a bra: __ Yes   __ No   __ Depends on the dress

I want a second dress for the reception: __ Yes   __ No

I prefer: Classic Silhouette   1   2   3   4   5   6   7   8   9   10   Bold Silhouette

I envision: Simple Details   1   2   3   4   5   6   7   8   9   10   Elaborate Details

I care more about: Appearance   1   2   3   4   5   6   7   8   9   10   Comfort

I am feeling: Modest   1   2   3   4   5   6   7   8   9   10   Brave

My favorite necklines: _____

My favorite silhouettes: _____

AFTER YOU START SHOPPING

Color(s) that look good on my skin: __ White   __ Off-White   __ Bold color (_____)

I actually like: Simple Details   1   2   3   4   5   6   7   8   9   10   Elaborate Details

I now care about: Appearance   1   2   3   4   5   6   7   8   9   10   Comfort

I am feeling: Modest   1   2   3   4   5   6   7   8   9   10   Brave

My favorite necklines: _____

My favorite silhouettes: _____

GOWN SILHOUETTES

 column

 flowy sheath

 structured sheath

 fit & flare

 trumpet

 mermaid

 high-low

 ball gown
drop waist + princess skirt

 structured A-line

 flowy A-line

 drop-waist + full skirt

WEDDING GOWN DISCUSSION TOPICS

fabric and other materials, their color and texture
silhouette, sleeves, neckline, waist, hem length, train length, bustle
appliques, rhinestones, bead work, bows, embellishments
accessories, foundation garments, undergarments, shoe height
ease of movement while wearing gown, ability to sit
steaming prior to wedding, preservation after wedding
cleaning and emergency stain removal
turnaround time from order date
deposit, balance due, cost of alterations, and group discounts

VEIL LENGTHS

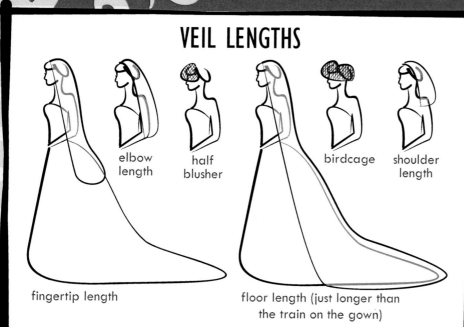

elbow length

half blusher

birdcage

shoulder length

fingertip length

floor length (just longer than the train on the gown)

BUSTLE OPTIONS FOR LONG TRAINS

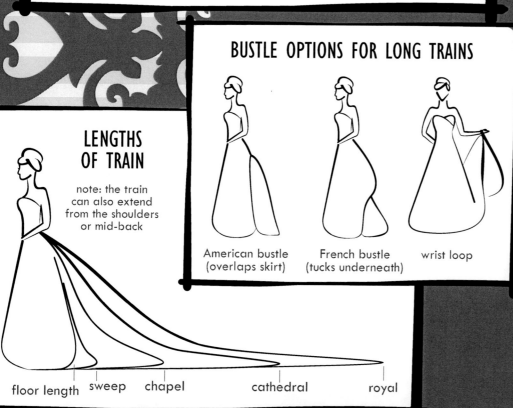

American bustle (overlaps skirt)

French bustle (tucks underneath)

wrist loop

LENGTHS OF TRAIN

note: the train can also extend from the shoulders or mid-back

floor length   sweep   chapel   cathedral   royal

BLUSHER: a veil that covers the face

DROP VEIL: the veil material has no gathers, fold or pleats

GATHERED VEIL: material is bunched in order to have more volume

MANTILLA VEIL: has a thick band of lace around the veil's border

VEIL MATERIALS: sheer fabric like tulle (pronounced *tool*), netting, or lace

AMERICAN BUSTLE: buttons the excess train over the top of the skirt and a sweep train remains

FRENCH BUSTLE: tucks the excess skirt underneath itself, fastens with ribbons, and can be very elaborate

WRIST LOOP: attaches the middle of the train to a bracelet

NECKLINES

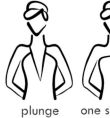

rounded sweetheart square scalloped scoop v-neck plunge one shoulder

rounded sweetheart square scalloped scoop with cowl neck v-neck plunge one shoulder

rounded sweetheart square scalloped scoop v-neck plunge one shoulder

rounded sweetheart square scalloped scoop v-neck plunge one shoulder

MORE NECKLINES

| rounded | sweetheart | square | scalloped | scoop | v-neck | plunge | one shoulder |

| rounded | sweetheart | square | scalloped | scoop | v-neck | plunge | one shoulder |

| peter pan | shirt | wing | shawl | mandarin | funnel | turtle neck | queen ann |

| racer front | bib | boat neck | rounded-up | key hole | wrap | pointed | criss-crossed |

3/4 SLEEVE AND LONG SLEEVE

HALTER

COLLARS

UNIQUE NECKLINES

51

BACKS

square

criss-cross
with scoop

halter
with deep-v

key-hole

racer

open

full coverage
or sheer back

zipper

buttons

corset

SKIRTS

full skirt

split front

tiered &
asymmetrical

pleated

pickups

gathered

ballerina

peplum

empire waist

ruffled

COVER-UPS

bolero

capelet

cardigan

cropped jacket

faux fur shrug

feather boa

hooded cape

muffler

poncho

shawl

sheer stole

wrap

SPECIFIC SLEEVES

fitted sleeves

Juliet sleeves

cap sleeves #1

long bishop sleeves   long bell sleeves

fitted sleeves

3/4 Juliet

cap sleeves #2   3/4 bishop sleeves   3/4 bell sleeves

shortsleeves

off-shoulder Juliet

cap sleeves #3

Snow White sleeves

short bell sleeves

WEDDING GOWN IDEA SKETCHES

TEN WAYS TO ~~IMPRESS~~ WORK WITH A BRIDAL GOWN CONSULTANT:

BEFORE YOU SHOW UP:

1. Timing is everything - if you are not yet engaged or if you plan on losing 20 pounds, it's not yet time to get fitted for a dress. One the filp-side, if you wait too long, then there will not be enough time for the dress to be made / customized / altered. Each store has their own time-line, which you can ask about before you book an appointment.

2. Book an appointment. Your consultant will take you more seriously and will be prepared to give you undivided attention.

3. Set your budget and stick to it. Don't waste your consultant's time on dresses / collections / designers that are not even an option.

4. Know the lingo - nothing is less helpful than asking for a "simple" or "elegant" wedding gown. That does not narrow it down.

ON THE DAY OF YOUR APPOINTMENT:

5. Take a shower - B.O. is hard to get out of a floor sample. So is blood.

SHOW UP ON TIME, AND THEN...

6. Wear foundation garments - bring your own or try on the samples that are available - it will effect the fit of your gown.

7. Try on different silhouettes and shades of white. That is the best way to see what flatters your body - not your imagination or a picture.

8. Know how you will pay and what terms and conditions come with the dress. Wedding dress retailers are not like other stores. Some shops require a 50% deposit, others want 100%. Do they offer refunds if you change your mind? Don't get blind-sided.

9. Ask about customization and alterations - they are NEVER free, and must be accounted for. They may not be able to give you a quote, but at least get a ballpark figure.

10. Write down your top favorites and your bridal size. Ask your consultant to call you when a sale is coming up. Then go sleep on it.

wedding party attire

COMMON ATTIRE CONCERNS

- Attendants, VIPs, and parents of the flower girl/ring bearer typically pay for their own attire/rental, with a few exceptions. If you want them in costume, you should cover the cost with your wedding budget. If you choose attire for your attendants that is more expensive than average, then it would be appropriate to split the cost. It varies, but in many places, average is $200 to $300 - including alterations and accessories.

- Junior bridesmaids and flower girls can match their grown-up counterparts, but they do not have to. They may wear a more modest version of the maids' dress or something completely different. See opposite page for ideas to tie the ensemble together.

BRIDESMAID DRESS LENGTHS

mini-skirt · knee-length · tea-length · floor-length · high-low

- Young attendants: Strapless dresses are not a good idea for little girls. Ring bearers can wear shorts.

- The dads can dress to match the Groom or choose their own attire that is on the same *Level of Fanciness* (see page 58) as the Groom.

- The moms and the female VIPs do not need to match the bridesmaids, but you can ask them to coordinate with the color scheme and theme. One option is to give them an accessory that coordinates with the attendants.

- Groomsmen can wear non-matching black suits and no one will notice. Matching ties and handkerchiefs (or other item) bring them together. See *Matching Items for Mismatched Men* on page 58 for more ideas.

- Give jobs to the flower girl and ring bearer that they can handle. For example, do not give a canine ring bearer the actual rings. You may want the flower girl to sprinkle petals evenly down the aisle, so have her practice or just accept that she may dump her petals on one spot. Have a plan with the parents about when & where the little attendants will get dressed & what to do if he/she/they have a meltdown.

- In your wedding invitation or on you wedding website, you can tell your guests if the attire is especially fancy or specific to your theme (such as black tie, beach formal, or western). Insider tip: no matter what you ask your guests to wear, someone will always show up in denim shorts.

BRIDESMAID COLOR SCHEMES

same color, same dress

same color, mismatched dresses

ombre color scheme, same dress

mismatched bridesmaids: different dresses,
same sash (or other matching item, see below)

MATCHING ITEMS FOR MISMATCHED BRIDESMAIDS

- sashes (worn at the waist or at the top of a strapless dress)
- belts (ribbon, metallic, or leather)
- shawls or scarves
- hats (in an outdoor setting)
- faux fur stoles or shrugs (winter)
- brooches or statement jewelry
- shoes or cowboy boots
- pin-on flowers or appliques
- hairdo or hairpin & makeup

FLOWER GIRL DRESS IDEAS

- dress to match the Bride
- dress to match the bridesmaids
- unique white dress
- color of dress that complements the bridesmaids
- unique dress and same sash (or other matching item) as the bridesmaids
- add a corsage to any dress

PREGNANT BRIDESMAID STRATEGIES

- choose an empire waist dress for all the bridesmaids, OR
- ask the pregnant bridesmaid to find a dress that matches the color and length of the other bridesmaid dresses, OR
- wait until the last minute to get her dress sized and purchased

MEN'S FORMALWEAR SPECTRUM OF FANCINESS

SWANKY "WHITE TIE"	FANCY "BLACK TIE"	FORMAL "BLACK TIE OPTIONAL"	SUNDAY BEST "SEMI-FORMAL"	TIE OPTIONAL "BUSINESS CASUAL"
white tuxedo with tails and gloves tophat for outdoors	black tuxedo with bow tie tophat optional	three-piece suit	suit with matching tie & handkerchief	navy blazer & khaki pant

MATCHING ITEMS FOR MISMATCHED MEN

- ties & handkerchiefs
- same color of collared shirts
- bowlers, fedoras, or top hats
- vests or cumber bunds
- bold belts
- shoes/boots
- sweaters (vests or cardigans)
- suspenders
- distinctive pants

RING BEARER ATTIRE IDEAS

- match the Groom or groomsmen
- any suit and tie
- dress clothes (with pants or shorts) with suspenders
- sailor costume

Dog/cat ring bearer:
- decorated collar
- bib "tuxedo"
- bow tie

ATTIRE NOTES

_____
_____
_____
_____
_____
_____
_____

BRIDESMAID IDEA SKETCHES

GROOMSMEN IDEA SKETCHES

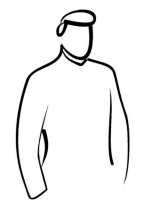   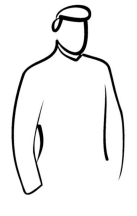

photography
and videography

After your wedding day is over, there are only one thing that will last as long your marriage: your wedding photography. The experts do not agree on the need for the photographer to be a professional. A pro does not need to be told to take a photo of the cake, but an amateur may do the work in lieu of a wedding gift. The bottom line: do what you, your betrothed, & your budget are comfortable with.

photographer discussion topics

Wedding Photography Skills
- Years and type of experience
- Equipment: cameras, lenses, filters, etc.
- Ask about wedding-related options: engagement portraits, boudoir session, videography, etc.
- Ask to see a sample album or presentation of a single wedding, start to finish, not just their portfolio
- Ask about their approach to the post-ceremony group photo process.

Videography Skills
- Years and type of experience
- Ask to see complete videos, not just highlights
- Look at the quality of the images, editing, special effects
- Listen for audio quality, dubbing, transitions
- Evaluate the completeness, style, and pace of the video.

Business Items to Discuss
- Package prices, a la carte prices, and extra hours cost
- Price of digital editing (beyond cropping, arranging in an album, etc.) and special effects
- Ownership of the license to the digital images
- Photographer's logo on the prints/digital images
- Contract terms and conditions, deposit and payment schedule, available dates, and travel arrangements
- Backup photographer/equipment, in case of emergency
- Who needs to be in the photos? You provide a list of group photos (see the *Example List: Group Photos*, opposite), must-have photos, and your wedding schedule, and incorporate feedback from the pro
- Recommendations for a videographer (if not included)

example list:
group photos

Before The Wedding

Groom, Groomsmen
Groom, his VIPs
Groom, Groom's Parents
Bride, Flower Girls
Bride, Bridesmaids
Bride, Bride's Mom
Bride, her VIPs

First look?
□ YES
□ NO

After The Ceremony

Bride, Groom, Bride's Parents
Bride, Groom, Bride's Immediate Family
Bride, Groom, Bride's Whole Family
Bride, Groom, Groom's Whole Family
Bride, Groom, Groom's Immediate Family
Bride, Groom, Groom's Parents
Bride, Groom, Bridal Party, Ushers
Bride, Groom, Bridesmaids, Groomsmen
Bride & Groom

Special Photo-Op Spot

Bride, Bridesmaids with prop (i.e. umbrellas)
Bride, Groom, Bridal Party
Bride & Groom

crafty bride
photography tip:

Get close to the camera to fill the frame with the subject (you and/or your Bridal Party). Stand far away to highlight an interesting background or capture a large number of people.

standing near the camera

standing near the background

tips for a rookie photographer

If you decide to use an amateur for your wedding photography, here are a few tips for that person to be effective. Hint: for better results – and less anxiety – use two photographers. Professionals do this for the same reasons.

What to Photograph
- Still Life - before the wedding and again before the reception, take wide shots of the venue. Get close-ups of the décor, the little details, and special tables.
- Portraits - solo & group photos, where the subjects pose (i.e. look at the camera & smile).
- Candids - without getting your subject's attention, take action shots of the events as they happen. Take both candid and posed shots of each event.

What to Bring
- Make a list with the couple of photos that they must have. Make a list of the group photos and put it in an order that flows. Bring these two lists. Review the *must have* list before hand, and use the *group photo* list when it's time to wrangle all the new in-laws.
- Tripod for low light, long exposures, and to use a timer.
- Extra camera, memory cards/film, & batteries. Keep gear in a fanny pack or other easy-access bag.
- Comfortable shoes. Professional attire, on the level of fanciness as the wedding.
- White sheet - for the couple to sit or stand upon (and keep their clothes clean) while they pose in nature.
- Mini-emergency kit. The couple will probably prepare one, but if you are out in a field taking portraits, then their sewing kit and tape won't be within arm's reach - but you are.
- Hint: cameras and equipment are available for rent in most places. Test all of the gear before the big day.

How to Proceed & Succeed
- Attend the rehearsal. Scope out the venue & the lighting. Get familiar with the wedding party. Talk to the attendants and parents about smiling down the aisle and when/where to pause for a picture.
- Talk to the officiant about where to stand, flash, and any rules/recommendations the venue may have.
- Talk to the couple about taking it slow (nerves can make people rush), especially during their first kiss, so you have time to do your job.
- Play with angle (i.e. move in a circle around the cake as you photograph it), your perspective (i.e. stand on a ladder to get shots of the whole room), & the depth of field (Hint: low aperture/F-stop makes the background out of focus).
- Shoot multiple images of everything. Use a rapid-fire setting (if your camera has it) during the kiss, the bouquet toss, & every event that happens fast.
- Stand on a chair during the group photos to reduce double-chins. Be assertive but nice to get subjects posed where every face is totally visible. Tell guests when they are free to leave for the reception.
- Use flash when you are in the sun (it's called fill flash) and in low light (unless using a tripod).
- Shoot on film ONLY if you have two cameras.

thrifty bride
do-it-yourself
"photo booth"

What you need...
• Digital camera (or video camera) and tripod on a table.
• Distinct backdrop.
• Props, such as a chalk board, picture frames, or silly hats.
• Instructions for taking "photo booth" photos
• Info cards with instructions for finding the photos online.

How to pull it off...
Place signs around the room pointing to the photo booth.
Leave instructions with the camera, such as:
   1. write a message to the newlyweds on the chalkboard,
   2. stand on the X,
   3. ask a fellow guest to take your photo, then return the favor
   4. take an info card and check the photo website next week.

Who makes it happen...
The DJ/emcee can remind guests to visit the "photo booth".
Ask a Helper to check on the photo booth periodically, collect
   props that go astray, check the camera battery, and to pack
   up the booth gear after the reception.

feisty bride
photography
tip:

Some of your guests will take pictures with their phones and digital cameras, which sounds great - to get extra candid shots and perspectives. But in the months after the wedding, I can be an hassle to get copies of their images.

For guests with digital cameras, set up a table with a computer and a card reader at the reception. Ask your guests to upload their digital photos before they depart. A Helper can encourage guests and help them with the computer.

For guests who take pics their phones, set up a hashtag or a website for their images. Tell your guests about it in the wedding program or with emcee announcements.

photography notes
_____

_____
_____
_____
_____
_____
_____
_____

Food & Drink

THE MODERN WEDDING RECEPTION REVOLVES AROUND EATING. GUESTS MAY SKIP THE DANCING OR THE TOASTS, BUT NO WEDDING GUEST SKIPS THE FOOD. THE TIME OF DAY AND THE SETTING NEED TO CORRESPOND WITH THE FOOD AND DRINK CHOICES. A RECEPTION THAT OVERLAPS A MEAL TIME SHOULD INCLUDE THAT MEAL AT SEATED TABLES. IF YOU SERVE ALCOHOL, THE LATER THE HOUR AND THE LONGER THE RECEPTION, THE MORE THE DRINKS WILL FLOW. AS THE MAJOR DESSERT, THE WEDDING CAKE DOUBLES AS THE FOCAL POINT OF THE RECEPTION.

Food & Stationery

Your RSVP card can help you plan for your reception food. You could ask your guests for their choice of meal, if they need a vegetarian option, or how many children are coming. Be careful with the wording, or else it could appear that you are serving children as a meal option.

Guests should be told ahead of time if your reception is a cocktail reception, full meal, B.Y.O.B, or just cake and punch. There is more info on this topic in the Reception Stationery section on page 26.

An informed guest is a happy guest. To avoid a mix-up, put menus or reception programs on the tables at the reception. An ample appetizer buffet, for example, may confuse guests into loading up on mini corn-dogs, which they believe to be lunch. Signs and announcement can also keep everyone in the know.

Food Selection for Guests

Your dinner fare can make or break a guest's experience at your reception. The couple's favorite dishes are common, but an exotic dinner can leave some guests feeling alienated (and hungry). The best approach is to offer plenty of choices.

Another way to consider your guests on a personal level is to ask about food allergies. To offer a vegetarian option is just the beginning. If a guest has celiac disease, then no part of their food can come in contact with gluten. If the dietary restrictions of individuals conflict too much with your vision, you are not obligated to place the restrictions on the whole reception. Specially prepared meals and dessert can be managed separately, as long as the chef knows the reason.

Ways to Serve Reception Fare

Meal Options

MULTI-COURSE MEAL WITH WAIT STAFF
having a waiter and lots of options pampers guests

BUFFET MEAL
guests feel free to meet their own needs, buffet style can take up a lot of room, and you may want a hired wait staff to clear the tables (therefore not necessarily cheaper)

FAMILY STYLE
works well with big tables and familiar guests but it can waste a lot of food

FOOD TRUCK
fine food served from a trailer... who knew?

Appetizer Options

SERVED APPETIZERS
when you have a wait staff

APPETIZER BUFFET
when guests will arrive hungry but need to wait for the bridal party to arrive

MULTIPLE APPETIZER STATIONS
to spread out the crowd and create movement

DO-IT-YOURSELF APPETIZER PROJECT
like a chocolate fountain, tacos, or fondue

APPETIZERS AS CENTERPIECES
put the appetizers to double duty

Drink Options

SOFT DRINKS
punch, coffee, sodas, iced tea, juice, and water

BEER & WINE
allows guests to toast without a full bar

CHAMPAGNE TOAST
can be included for the wedding party only

SIGNATURE COCKTAIL
the new trend - add some flair & a little booze

FULL BAR / CASH BAR
requires an array of alcohol, mixers, & a hired bartender; use an online alcohol calculator to help stock the bar

B.Y.O.B.
when you have a strong reason against serving alcohol but don't want to alienate the guests who do drink

Dessert Options

WEDDING CAKE & GROOM'S CAKE
a traditional way to give guests contrasting options

WEDDING CAKE WITH A DIFFERENT FLAVOR IN EACH TIER
to meet a variety of tastes with only one dessert

UNCONVENTIONAL DESSERT BUFFET
such as gourmet popcorn, cupcakes, pies, & cake balls or even ice cream, shaved ice, or s'mores

Food & Drink Professionals

Caterer Discussion Topics

~ availability and fees for waiters/meat carvers/bartenders/cleanup staff
~ availability and fees for table settings, linens, other rental items (if available)
~ the caterer's specialty & most popular dishes
~ in-season and local ingredient choices
~ charge for setting up and serving food & drink items provided by others
~ charge for reception set up (i.e. setting up tables & lighting candles)
~ do you need access to electricity, kitchen, or ice? will you bring a cook tent?
~ price difference for adding meal options or doing a buffet
~ sample menu tasting (date & cost)
~ head-count (including the officiant and reception vendors)
~ contract terms & payment due dates

Bartender Discussion Topics

~ fees: service, corkage, set up, tip jar, extra hours, clean up
~ supplies: ice, fruit, glassware, napkins, blender, margarita machine, pitchers
~ drink menu: selection of drinks, mixers, signature cocktail, brands of liquor
~ selection of soft (non-alcoholic) drinks
~ liquor delivery/pickup and return of unopened bottles
~ decide on the policy for serving drinks to the other vendors at the reception

Self~Catering Considerations

~ setup/cleanup staff or Helpers... who washes the dishes?
~ the time necessary to do all the prep and cooking
~ how long the foods will be fresh after their preparation
~ how to keep hot food hot and how to keep cold food cold
~ advance preparation/freezing/outsourcing certain portions
~ rental options for serving utensils, serving platters, chafing dishes, & coolers

Notes

The Cake

THE WEDDING CAKE HAS BECOME MORE THAN JUST DESSERT - IT MAY BE AN EDIBLE WORK OF ART, A SYMBOL OF THE BRIDE & GROOM, OR A CONVERSATION PIECE. THE TERM "CAKE" IS BEING USED VERY LOOSELY, AS ALL KINDS OF CONFECTIONS ARE GOING INTO THE CONSTRUCTION. AS LONG AS YOU PROVIDE DESSERT, YOUR GUESTS WILL BE HAPPY.

Cake Discussion Topics

FLAVORS
~ *schedule a tasting (which may cost extra) with each potential bakery to try their cake, filling, and frosting flavors*
~ *ask about their specialty flavors and seasonal ingredients*
~ *ask how the bakery might accommodate dietary and allergy restrictions*
~ *remember that guests care more about the taste of the dessert than the appearance or presentation*

FROSTING & DECORATIONS
~ *bring your wedding colors, photos of your wedding gown & bridesmaids' dresses, and your wedding notebook*
~ *have a general idea of how you want your cake to look (colors, style, size, shape)*
~ *cake topper ideas: figurines, hearts, monograms, rings, flowers (real or sugar), fruit, or a family heirloom*
~ *frosting options: buttercream, fondant, marzipan, whipped frosting, royal icing, gum paste, glazes, ganache*
~ *note: certain frosting (depending on the recipe) can melt right off - tell the baker if cake will be displayed outdoors*

BUSINESS ITEMS
~ *discuss the budget for the cake, number of servings, variety and types of desserts to be served, and fake tiers*
~ *pricing structure and fees for delivery, insurance, set up, cake service, and cleanup*
~ *wedding day schedule, contract terms, cancellation policy, deposit, taxes, and payment schedule*
~ *rental items: tables, linens, plates, knife & server, utensils, toasting glasses, cake stands, centerpieces, props*
~ *plan for saving the top layer or a slice of cake for your first anniversary*
~ *giving away confections as wedding favors, boxing up leftover cake for guests*

DO-IT-YOURSELF WEDDING CAKE CONSIDERATIONS
~ *ingredients: availability, shelf-life, make-ahead timeline, storage, and cost*
~ *tools: can you borrow or rent some of the baking tools? what implements do you want to own forever?*
~ *recipes: do you know where to buy and the costs of the ingredients in your recipes? have you made them before?*
~ *density: a dense cake is more stackable than an airy cake. try adding pudding mix or sour cream to your recipe*
~ *logistics: how to assemble, store, and transport a big cake. Can you assemble it at the reception venue?*
~ *skills: do you have the confidence & time enough to practice the skills required to make your dream cake?*

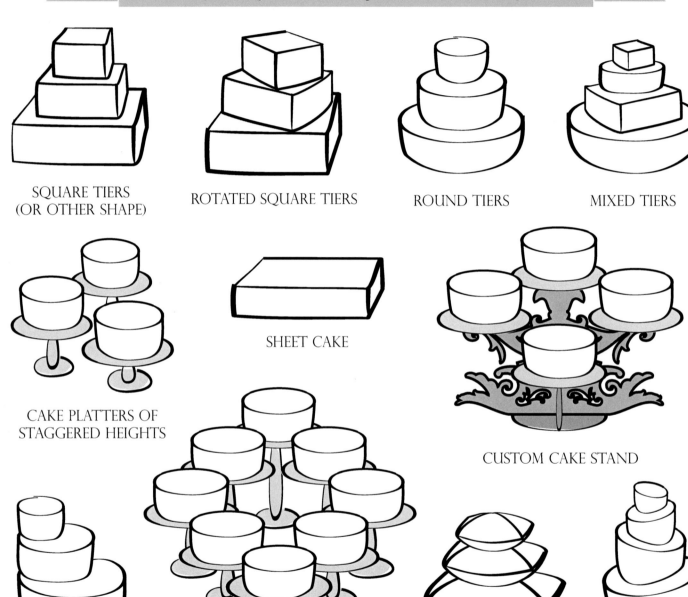

Examples of Wedding Cake Shapes

SQUARE TIERS
(OR OTHER SHAPE)

ROTATED SQUARE TIERS

ROUND TIERS

MIXED TIERS

CAKE PLATTERS OF
STAGGERED HEIGHTS

SHEET CAKE

CUSTOM CAKE STAND

STAIR STEPS

ARRANGED CAKE PLATTERS

PILLOW-SHAPED TIERS

TOPSY-TURVY

Baking a Wedding Cake

Interior of a Tiered Cake

HERE'S A DOOZIE OF AN IDEA: BAKE YOUR OWN WEDDING CAKE. DOES THAT SCARE YOU OR EXCITE YOU? IF YOU ARE STILL READING, THEN THE FOLLOWING PAGES ARE FOR YOU.

MAKING A WEDDING CAKE IS A COMBINES SEVERAL SKILLS: BAKING, ENGINEERING, AND ARTISTRY. IT IS NOT SOMETHING TO BE TAKEN LIGHTLY, BUT IT IS POSSIBLE.

THERE ARE ALSO A LOT OF MATERIALS THAT ARE REQUIRED: THE INGREDIENTS, THE BAKEWARE, THE DECORATING TOOLS AND CONSTRUCTION MATERIALS. NOT TO MENTION STORAGE SPACE AND A TOPPER! STILL READING? THEN DIVE IN!

HELPFUL CAKE SEARCH TERMS

~ *wedding cake tutorial*
~ *frosting decorating tips*
~ *cake batter amounts*
~ *wedding cake frosting*
~ *tiered wedding cake*
~ *dense wedding cake*
~ *how to store a cake*

SMALL LAYER, UPSIDE-DOWN
filling
LAYER OF SMALL SIZE CAKE
filling
LAYER OF SMALL SIZE CAKE
a smear of frosting
CAKE CIRCLE
DOWEL RODS
MEDIUM LAYER, UPSIDE-DOWN
filling
LAYER OF MEDIUM SIZE CAKE
filling
LAYER OF MEDIUM SIZE CAKE
a smear of frosting
CAKE CIRCLE
DOWEL RODS
LARGE LAYER, UPSIDE-DOWN
filling
LAYER OF LARGE SIZE CAKE
filling
LAYER OF LARGE SIZE CAKE
a smear of frosting
CAKE CIRCLE
CAKE PLATTER/DISPLAY
ONE DOWEL ROD THROUGH THE ENTIRE CAKE (NOT PICTURED)

Step~By~Step Cake Instructions

BEFORE YOU BAKE

~ *level your oven(s) and place the rack in the center. Make sure the pans fit inside. You can bake two pans at the same time on the same rack, but only if they fit with space to spare.*

~ *prep your cake pans with a parchment paper liner, cut to lay flat on the bottom of the pan. Grease the sides of the pan.*

~ *give your oven(s) time to preheat. Use an oven thermometer to confirm temperature.*

MIX IT UP

~ *make enough batter to bake an extra layer for each tier - just in case! follow your recipe, and take note of any changes.*

~ *do not save unused batter for another day.*

~ *measure out the batter and fill cake pans with 1" of batter. Spread thick batter with a spatula to the edges of the pan.*

~ *bake your cake layers at 325°F (163°C). A higher oven temperature can lead to a taller dome and can cause cracks to form. Five to ten minutes after the recommended bake time, insert a wooden toothpick in the center of the cake. Keep the oven closed while you do this. The cake is done when the toothpick comes out clean. If not, bake for five to ten more minutes and check again. You may also notice the cake making a light crackling sound - this is louder and more active when the cake is halfway baked, then it calms down when the cake is done.*

PREP THE CAKES

~ *after baking, set the cake and pan on a cooling rack. Run a sharp knife along the edges of the pan. After the cake has cooled in the pan at least thirty minutes, put a cooling rack over the top of the cake pan and flip them over together. Peel the paper off of the bottom of the cake, then turn the cake right-side-up onto a cooling rack.*

~ *allow cake to cool completely, even overnight. Level each layer with a cake leveler or a long, serrated knife and height guides (such as cans of tuna fish). (HINT: the cake from the domes that gets sawed off can be used for cake balls.) Use some frosting to stick the bottom layer of cake to the cake circle. Assemble each tier using the layers, filling, and cake circle (see opposite). The cake circle should be the same diameter at the cake above it, so that you can hide the seam on the finished cake. Note: if your filling is something other than frosting or ganache, then frost the tops & bottoms of every layer of cake before assembly to keep them from getting soggy.*

~ *if you designed a naked cake, brush the exposed cake edges with simple syrup to keep the cake from drying out.*

~ *apply a thin coat of frosting that will not be seen, called the crumb layer. The crumb layer keeps the cake fresh and the crumbs contained. Refrigerate uncovered until the crumb layer hardens, then smooth any sharp points in the frosting. Wrap each tier in plastic wrap and freeze for up to four months or refrigerate up to a week prior to decorating.*

DECORATING

~ *frozen cakes do not need to thaw before being assembled and decorated. Allow time for your finished cake to thaw before serving, which can take up to four hours.*

continued →

DECORATING *(continued)*

~ *frost each of the tiers separately. Start at the top of the tier and work the frosting downward. If frosting becomes too sticky or runny, stop and refrigerate the frosting for fifteen minutes. If frosting is too thick to spread (while at room temperature), add corn syrup a little at a time until you reach the desired consistency.*

~ *use a hot metal spatula to put the finishing touches on the frosting's surface. Periodically run hot water over the spatula, dry it off, and continue smoothing the edges of the cake.*

~ *insert dowels (or hollow cylinders) through each tier, cutting them to match the height of the top of the finished frosting. If the cake topper is heavy, then put dowels in the top tier of cake as well.*

~ *in the interest of refrigerator space, you may choose to assemble the cake at the reception site, leaving the final touches to the day of or the day before the wedding.*

~ *to store the cake(s) in a refrigerator, put them in a sealed container or a cardboard box, to keep the funky fridge smells from permeating into the cake. If boxes are not available, then refrigerate the cake until the decorations are hardened, then drape lightly with plastic wrap.*

~ *finished cakes may be stored at room temperature for 24-48 hours, depending on the type of frosting.*

~ *consult with your florist about putting real flowers on your cake. Flower stems can leak fluids that are bitter or unsafe to consume, and some species of flowers can drop bright yellow pollen all over your frosting.*

WHAT TO LOOK FOR WHEN BAKING A PRACTICE CAKE

~ *volume of batter created by your recipe*
~ *amount of time needed to bake at 325ºF*
~ *the thickness of a layer of baked cake created by 1" of batter*
~ *taste and texture of the cake*
~ *density of the cake (will it stack well?)*

Cake Advice

FOR THE CRAFTY BRIDE

~ *decorating a wedding cake is harder than baking a wedding cake, and the best way to excel is to watch tutorials online or to take cake decorating classes (at a bakery or craft store), then use any excuse to practice your skills. It's Arbor Day? Bake and frost a cake, then take it to work.*

~ *explore the full range of frosting and edible cake décor - like gum paste, marzipan, shimmer dust.*

FOR THE THRIFTY BRIDE

~ *rent the really big cake pans from a bakery, cake supply store, or caterer.*

~ *borrow any tools that are available.*

~ *ingredients - especially fruits - go in and out of season, so choose ingredients that will be abundantly available (and cheap) during your wedding season.*

FOR THE FEISTY BRIDE

~ *when frosting a wedding cake, it's more difficult to create smooth edges and perfectly consistent piping. Instead, create textures over your frosting with items such as: coconut flakes, bonbons, slivered almonds, rock candy, white chocolate curls, vertical strips of fondant, or drizzled white chocolate.*

~ *decorating the seams (which hides the cake circles) can made or break the appearance of a wedding cake. The key is to be consistent. If you are using frosting, use a piping bag & decorating tips to create a string of pearls, rosettes, stars, shells, etc. An alternative to frosting is to cover the seams with sweets that are consistent in size and shape, such as truffles, Jordan almonds, or round candies.*

the Ceremony

This is what you've been waiting for - to get married! In most places, the Ceremony must legally include the couple, the officiant, and some witnesses. The couple states that they intend to marry one another, say I do, a paper is signed, and done. If you want more than that, you have lots of options. The content of a Wedding Ceremony varies widely with culture, religion, tradition, and personal preference. Here are some things to consider when you choose your Officiant, book the Ceremony Venue, and create the Order of Events.

Tone of the Ceremony

indoor or outdoor
long or short
religious or civil
solemn or silly
universal or self-written
audience participation or silence
reflecting on the past or looking forward
moved to tears or peals of laughter
simple or elaborate

Role of the Officiant

Words of Welcome: scripted or improvised
Vows: repeat-after-me or hand over the microphone
Reflection: prayerful or practical
Readings: scripture or poetry
Where to stand at the altar/podium/archway/stage
Microphone: lapel, handheld, on a stand, or none
Timing of events and announcements
Marriage License: when and where it gets signed

Example Order of Events

Entrance of couple's grandparents
Entrance of couple's parents
Entrance of Groom & Officiant
Entrance of the Bridal Party
Entrance of the Bride & her father/escort
Welcome
Expression of Intent
Readings/Traditional Event
Moment of Silence for departed loved ones
Reflection/Sermon
Unity Ceremony (candle, sand, handfasting, etc.)
Vows
Exchange of Rings
Pronouncement
Kiss
Exit Procession

Ceremony Music

live performance, recorded music, or both
a capella or accompaniment
acoustic or electric
classical or modern
number of musicians/vocalists
amount of room necessary for equipment
electrical outlet locations

Jobs to be Done

Ceremony Setup. Unload and place the traditional fixtures, programs, sign-in table, chairs, and altar. Arrange the programs, flowers, and décor. Wire-up and test the sound system. (Hint: take photos of any pre-existing damage that you find in the venue and on rental items... just in case you get blamed for it).

Get dressed. The **Wedding Gown Helper** will button/zip/lace up the back of the wedding gown, buckle the Bride's shoes, help the Bride go to the restroom, etc.

Gussy up. If you get dressed and ready offsite, keep your makeup with you. Do a quick touch-up before the ceremony and again before pictures, in case of crying, kissing, or sweating.

Distribute Flowers. Each bouquet, boutonniere, and corsage ends up with/pinned to the right person.

Kid Jockey keeps flower girls and ring bearers together & entertained before the ceremony.

Dressing Room Steward will make sure the wedding party does not leave anything behind. This person can keep up with the emergency kit and the Bridal Party's purses during the ceremony.

Take a Headcount. Check that everyone in the Bridal Party and procession is present or accounted for.

Greeters hand out ceremony programs and direct guests to the sign-in table.

Ushers seat your guests as they arrive at the ceremony. They officially begin the ceremony by seating the couple's grandparents and parents.

Director/Coordinator give the cues to the musicians, Officiant, and Bridal Party.

Readers take part in the ceremony by reading a poem, scripture, or passage.

Photographer wrangles the Bridal Party and family into the various group photos.

Getaway Car Chauffeur drives the Newlyweds from the ceremony to the reception.

Takedown all the fixtures and décor and pack them up. Clean up the venues and take inventory of any damage. Deliver décor to where it belongs.

Special Ceremony Ideas

For the Crafty Bride:
an offbeat unity ceremony can be very crafty, like painting or building something together, planting a "unity tree," or literally tying the knot out of a rope.

For the Thrifty Bride:
incorporate items into the ceremony that can be used again. For example, instead of buying a one-time-use ring pillow, tie the rings to a meaningful book.

For the Feisty Bride:
plan a dramatic entrance (such as a curtain of flowers parting for you and your escort) or an unusual entrance song.

Savor your Ceremony

- Allow ample time to get ready so that you don't feel rushed. Do your best to start the Ceremony on time (or close to it), so the events can get off on the right foot.

- Focus on relationships. Tell your friends, family, and Groom how much you love them. Use the words "thank you" as often as you can. Take the time to say a prayer.

- Once you have your makeup on, you are not the right person to fix a problem. The Coordinator or a member of your Bridal Party should handle all surprises and hiccups in the plans. Know ahead of time who can be trusted to solve problems on your behalf.

- Nothing can ruin the mood at a wedding quite like a Bride's tantrum. If you feel one coming on, instead of murdering everyone in sight, find some privacy. Run in place for a minute (not in your high heels), or cool off with some deep breathing. It's better to be late and calm than to be on time and upset.

Ceremony Notes

_____
_____
_____
_____
_____
_____
_____
_____

Order of Events

_____
_____
_____
_____
_____
_____
_____

Officiant

_____
_____
_____
_____
_____

Jobs to be Done

_____
_____
_____
_____

Ceremony Music

_____
_____
_____
_____

DRESSING ROOM PACKING LIST

It is better to have this stuff and not need it than to need it and not have it.

PREPARATION LEVEL ALPHA:
Hygiene & Attire
- toothbrush, toothpaste, & mouthwash
- deodorant, perfume, razor, & tissues
- bouquets
- foundation garments, gown, & shoes
- veil, garter, & jewelry
- the groom's wedding ring

PREPARATION LEVEL BETA:
Hair & Makeup
- makeup necessities: eyes, lips, cheeks, concealer, powder, etc.
- hair spray, curling/flat iron, hair pins/combs/elastics/headbands
- nail polish, nail file, & polish remover
- cotton balls/swabs, tweezers
- petroleum jelly & baby powder

PREPARATION LEVEL GAMMA:
Contact with the Outside World
- Bridal Party & vendor contact list
- cell phone & charger
- camera

PREPARATION LEVEL DELTA:
Relaxation & Fun
- gift/letter to the groom (from the bride)
- music player
- prayer book or journal
- Champagne & glasses

EMERGENCY LEVEL ALPHA:
Sweating, Crying, & Kissing
(keep in the Bride's or MOH's purse)
- touch-up makeup & hand mirror
- tissues
- hair pins
- breath mints/spray

EMERGENCY LEVEL BETA:
Medical(ish) Issues
- painkillers, bandages, antacid, glucose tabs, smelling salts, allergy meds, etc.
- pads/tampons, lotion, eye drops
- bottled water, straws, & snacks

EMERGENCY LEVEL GAMMA:
Wardrobe Malfunctions
- stain remover/chalk, dryer sheets
- extra hosiery, bra straps, etc.
- safety pins & sewing kit
- double-sided tape & florist tape
- lint roller (+ one for the groom)
- scissors, super glue, & duct tape

EMERGENCY LEVEL DELTA:
Weather & Nature
- sunscreen & insect repellant
- umbrellas
- hand fans
- hand sanitizer/wet wipes

The Reception

Time to celebrate! The Reception is an opportunity to showcase your personality, creativity, and dance moves. When you arrive, the hard part is over, the nerves have calmed, and you have your Groom at your side. Then you get to savor the fruits of your labor and to enjoy the attention of your friends and family.

Immediately after the Ceremony, you may be caught up with the photographer, so the beginning of the Reception is a sort of transition time. Give your guests something to eat and activities for them to do, such as games to play, a crafty place to leave advice for the newlyweds, and/or a photo booth to enjoy.

Once you arrive, you have until the end of the Reception to greet your guests and thank them for coming. Some couples choose to do a receiving line, or they may visit with each table during dinner. If you miss anyone, the Groom's toast is a good time to express your gratitude towards all of your guests for their attendance. If a guest is overly chatty, you can say something like, "Sorry to interrupt, but I MUST dance to this song. Will you come do the Chicken Dance with me?"

Take time for yourself, so that you don't get dehydrated, overwhelmed, drunk, faint, or otherwise cause a scene. If things don't go according to plan, shrug it off and make things work as best you can. Rely on your bridal party to handle any issues. You may not get a moment alone with your Groom, so be sure to check in with him periodically for a kiss or a squeeze of the hand.

Reception Activity Ideas

FOR THE CRAFTY BRIDE

Create a customized lawn game (like croquet or a bean bag toss) with your new monogram. The game can entertain guests at your house parties for years to come.

FOR THE THRIFTY BRIDE

Create an "I Spy" game. Print out a few copies per table. Provide a way for guests to upload or share those photos online.

FOR THE FEISTY BRIDE

Play the Shoe Game with your Groom. Sit back to back and hold one of each of your shoes. Ask guests to submit questions like, *Who is the better driver?* Answer by holding up a shoe.

Example Order of Events

Group & Bridal Party photos (immediately following the Ceremony)

Guests begin to arrive at Reception Venue, greeted by appetizers .... Soft, upbeat background music

DJ announces that the bar is open

Cocktail & Activity Hour [games and photo booth] .... Oldies music mix

DJ announces the arrival of the Bridal Party .... "Good Riddance" by Green Day

Bride & Groom enter and go immediately to into the First Dance .... "At Last" by Etta James

DJ announces that the dance floor is open. Dancing/Mingle Time .... Country dance music mix

Simultaneous Father-Daughter dance and Mother-Son dance .... "What a Wonderful World" by Louis Armstrong

DJ announces that dinner is served and reminder about photo booth

Bride and Groom eat with the Bridal Party and then visit each guest table for a quick *hello* .... Non-dancing song mix

Toasts: Groom, Father of the Bride, Best Man, and Maid of Honor .... Soft, classical background music

Cake cutting, cake and coffee are served .... "Sweet Caroline" by Neil Diamond

Dancing/Mingle Time .... Start dance mix with "Let's Get it Started" by Black Eyed Peas

Bouquet Toss and Garter Toss [then Bride changes outfit] .... "Brick House" by The Commodores

Dancing/Mingle Time .... Dance music mix

DJ announces the Last Song .... "The Dance" by Garth Brooks

Grand Exit of the Bride & Groom with sparklers .... "Beautiful Day" by U2

Cleanup time, vendors to exit the Reception venue by 11pm

Music Plan

Musician/DJ/Emcee Discussion Topics

Must-have Songs for the "Must-Play" Song List and when to play them (Hint: your favorite songs that are not dance tunes may be good for cocktail hour or dinner time)

Songs, content, and genres on the "Do Not Play" Song List (i.e. songs that mention *doing it* or the Cotton Eye Joe)

How to incorporate your Traditional songs

Announcements to make and when to make them

Contract & payment terms

Suggestions for the Ceremony Schedule (based on experience)

Helpful Search Terms

Reception Music
Wedding Reception Activities
Receiving Line
Reception Schedule
Cocktail Hour Fun
Wedding Toast
Reception Games

Reception Planning Questions

When will you have access to the Reception venue?

_____

Who will help with the set-up?

_____

How will you arrange tables and fixtures to encourage guests to use the entire space?

_____

How much time will you have at the venue and how do you want to use it?

_____

How much emphasis will there be on the food, cake, and drinks?

_____

How will the guests learn about special activities, find the restrooms, and how to sign in?

_____

Are music and dancing a high priority or a low priority?

_____

How will you make time to greet each of your guests (or as many as possible)?

_____

Who will be giving toasts (or speeches), and how much time will each person get?

_____

How will you encourage the celebratory mood (other than with alcohol)?

_____

What will the non-dancing guests do with their time?

_____

Do you wish to honor or remember any special guests?

_____

How late do you expect your guests to stay at the Reception?

_____

Who is in charge of keeping the Reception on schedule (i.e. emcee, DJ, or Wedding Coordinator)?

_____

How will you make your grand exit/sendoff (such as bubbles, sparklers, or helicopter getaway)?

_____

Who is in charge of the getaway car and will you use a chauffeur?

_____

Who will break down and clean up the venue?

_____

Which décor items are your property and where do they need to go?

_____

Where do the rented items need to go?

_____

Who will keep track of the tip envelopes and pass them to the vendors?

_____

Reception Notes

Activities

_____
_____
_____
_____
_____

Order of Events

_____
_____
_____
_____
_____
_____
_____
_____

Vendors

_____
_____
_____

Jobs to be Done

_____
_____
_____

Reception Music

_____
_____
_____
_____

Traditional Roles

The funny thing about traditions is that they change, and sometimes they change quickly. They also vary by culture. The following Traditional Roles encompass the typical American wedding activities and persons involved. There may be more or less items that you expect. There is no obligation to follow these lists, and the wedding police won't come knocking if you divvy up these tasks in another way.

Parents of the Bride

- The parents of the bride may host an engagement party for the Bride and Groom among their friends and family.
- They make the effort to meet the Groom's parents, if they have not already.
- In fading tradition, the Bride's parents host (plan and pay for) the wedding. More often these days, they contribute financially as they are able and host in the sense that their names are on the top of the invitation.
- The Mother of the Bride is next in line to plan the wedding, if the Bride is not interested or able. If not planning the wedding, she is expected to help make selections and support the Bride in them.
- The Bride's parents help choose the Circle of Invitees (more on page 19) and number of guests. They help track down addresses for the invitations. They help make the guest list for the bridal shower, but they are not to host it.
- The Mother of the Bride chooses wedding day attire that coordinates with the bridal party.
- The Father of the Bride wears wedding day attire that matches the Groom (more on page 58).
- The Father of the Bride walks the Bride down the aisle. A Bride can include her mother as a second escort. If her father is not able, another person of honor can escort her.
- The Mother of the Bride may participate in the unity ceremony (i.e. lighting one of the candles).
- The Father of the Bride gives a speech or toast at the wedding reception.

Parents of the Groom

- The parents of the Groom may host an engagement party for the Bride and Groom among their friends and family.
- In fading tradition, the Groom's parents host (plan and pay for) the rehearsal dinner. This may be related to the other fading tradition that the wedding is in the Bride's home town and so most of the out-of-town guests belong to the Groom's family. These days, the Groom's parents contribute as they are able to the cost of the entire wedding. The planning of the rehearsal dinner may get lumped in with the wedding planning.
- The Groom's parents contribute to the guest list. They help track down addresses for the invitations.
- The Mother of the Groom coordinates her wedding attire with the Mother of the Bride, so as not to clash.
- The Father of the Groom wears wedding day attire on the Groom's level of fanciness (more on page 58).
- The Mother of the Groom participates in the unity ceremony (i.e. lighting one of the candles).

Maid of Honor

- The Maid/Matron of Honor (A.K.A. Honor Attendant) is captain of the team of ladies who support the Bride.
- She helps the Bride to select the attire for the female attendants and organizes group fittings and spreads the word on how the maids are to get outfitted.
- She pays for her own travel and attire.
- The Maid of Honor may host the bridal shower, but this duty could go to an extended family member or family friend. The host of the showers spread the word about the Bride & Groom's gift registries. The Maid of Honor should try to attend each shower.
- She hosts the bachelorette party and/or lingerie shower. She may enlist the Bridesmaids as co-hosts.
- She must attend the weddindg rehearsal.
- She may give a toast/speech at the rehearsal dinner or the weding reception.
- On the wedding day, she will accompany the Bride in her preparations. Attend to the Bride's needs and whims.
- She holds the Groom's wedding ring (if there is no ring bearer) and the Bride's bouquet during the ceremony.
- She signs the marriage license as a witness
- The entire bridal party poses for photographs.
- At the reception, the Maid of Honor may stand in the receiving line and sit at the head table.

Flower Girl

- One or several little girls may serve as Flower Girl.
- The parents of the Flower Girl pay for her travel and attire.
- She attends the rehearsal and arrives early to the wedding.
- The Flower Girl walks down the aisle during the procession, just before the Bride and her escort. The Flower Girl carries a basket with flower petals, which she is to sprinkle on the aisle as she walks. She may carry a bouquet, if it is an honorary position.
- The Flower Girl poses for photographs with the bridal party.

The Best Man

- The Best Man hosts the bachelor party. He may enlist help from the Groomsmen. He should honor the Bride and Groom's wishes about content therein. He should try to attend any co-ed showers.
- He pays for his own travel and wedding day attire.
- All the Groomsmen help with setup if they are needed.
- He must attend the wedding rehearsal.
- The Best Man may give a toast/speech at the rehearsal dinner or the wedding reception.
- On the wedding day, he and the Groomsmen attend to the Groom's needs and whims. The Best Man holds the Bride's wedding ring (if there is no ring bearer).
- He signs the marriage license as a witness.
- At the reception, the Best Man may stand in the receiving line and sit at the head table.
- He poses for photographs with the bridal party.
- He may take on some of the Helper roles.

Ring Bearer

- The Ring Bearer is traditionally a boy, but of course a girl or can serve in this role... or even a pet.
- The parents of the Ring Bearer pay for his travel and attire.
- He must attend the rehearsal and arrive early to the wedding ceremony.
- The Ring Bearer walks down the aisle during the procession, holding a pillow or other object that has the wedding rings attached to it. He may carry fake rings, if it is an honorary position.
- The Ring Bearer poses for photographs with the bridal party.
- If the Ring Bearer is a pet, then these items apply to the animal's handler.

continued →

Bridesmaids

- Assist the Bride and Maid of Honor. Bridesmaids may help host the bridal shower. They should try to attend all showers.
- They pay for their own travel and wedding day attire.
- They must attend the wedding rehearsal and the rehearsal dinner.
- If the Bride and Groom need help with setup, they should try to contribute.
- On the wedding day, the bridesmaids attend to the Bride's needs and whims.
- During the ceremony, they stand alongside the Bride, with the Maid of Honor nearest to her.
- The entire bridal party poses for photographs.
- At the reception, the bridesmaids may stand in the receiving line and sit at the head table.
- They should encourage guests to enjoy the planned activities of the reception (including dancing and catching the bouquet).
- They may take on some of the Helper roles.

VIPs and Helpers

- The VIPs may be persons of honor - like grandparents of the Bride and Groom - or Helpers who get in the spotlight - like readers.
- Those VIPs and Helpers who participate in the ceremony should attend the wedding rehearsal.
- Helpers who do not participate in the ceremony should get written instructions outlining their duties.
- Tell the VIPs the wedding colors so they can dress in colors that do not clash with the bridal party.
- The VIPs might wear a corsage or boutonniere on the wedding day.
- Helpers perform some sort of duty (more on page 4) to help the Bride and Groom with the wedding. They should be honored with a thank you gift and/or note.

Groomsmen

- The groomsmen coordinate with the Groom and best man for their wedding day attire.
- They pay for their own travel and wedding day attire.
- Groomsmen typically attend the bachelor party and any co-ed bridal showers. They may help host the bachelor party.
- They help the Groom and best man with any wedding preparation tasks.
- Groomsmen attend the wedding rehearsal and the rehearsal dinner.
- They must arrive early to the wedding ceremony.
- The groomsmen stand alongside the Groom during the ceremony, with the best man nearest to him.
- The entire bridal party poses for photographs.
- At the reception, the groomsmen may stand in the receiving line and sit at the head table.
- They should encourage guests to enjoy the planned activities of the reception (including dancing and catching the garter).
- They may take on some of the Helper roles.

Ushers

- The Ushers' main duty is to help seat the guests at the wedding, according to whatever plan is in place.
- The ceremony begins when the Ushers seat the Bride and Groom's grandparents.
- They select wedding day attire that is formal and color coordinated to the wedding party.
- They must arrive early to the wedding ceremony.
- They may pass out programs to the wedding guests and unfurl the aisle runner.
- They encourage guests to enjoy the planned activities of the reception (including dancing and catching the garter).
- They may take on some of the Helper roles.

The Gift Registry

How to Create a Great Registry

1. Ask friends about their experiences with their gift registries. Review popular stores & websites. Consider your guests and their access to these retailers.

2. Choose between two and four locales.

3. Imagine your future home décor. Discuss your vision and houseware needs with your fiancé before registering.

4. Make your in-store experience more pleasant: Allow plenty of time. Avoid the store's busy times/days. Wear comfortable shoes, drink water, & bring a snack. Take a break if you get tired.

5. Register for offbeat items (such as hobby supplies, power tools, tech items, and gourmet ingredients) as well as the standard items (like dishes, linens, and home décor).

6. Include a wide range of price points.

7. Spread the word about your registries indirectly: on your wedding website or through your bridal shower. Never mention your registry in the wedding invitation.

8. Update your registries before and after the bridal shower(s).

9. Transfer any remaining items to your Birthday/Christmas wish list.

Fun Gift Registry Ideas

Crafty

sewing machine
stand mixer
barbecue grill
home brew kit
oil paint & supplies
vinyl plotter

Thrifty

Honeymoon excursions
concert / movie tickets
deep freezer
potted herbs
wine-of-the-month
membership

Feisty

lingerie
wine/keg refrigerator
winter coats
digital camera
canoe or bicycles
board games

Honeymoon

Destination Discussion Questions

Start with a focus and go from there. Would you like to experience wine country? Scuba diving? History? Spelunking? All of these?

Consider the season of your Honeymoon before choosing your destination and making your budget. Will it be hurricane season or the height of the tourist season?

Do you have a passport? With international travel, you must apply for passports at least three months in advance or pay extra. Check to see if you will need a visa or vaccines. Unless there are several months between the Wedding and Honeymoon, you will have to put the Bride's maiden name on the passport and plane tickets.

Will the destination be a surprise for the Bride? At least tell her what climate and activity level to expect and pack for.

Duration Discussion Questions

How much time off can you take off from your business/employer? (Hint: ask for this time as early as you can).

For travel across several time zones, consider plane time and jet lag time as separate from actual Honeymoon time.

Budget Discussion Questions

For your flights, booking early is key to low prices, direct flights, and short layovers.

What do you want to do while you visit your destination(s)? Tours, excursions, motor craft rentals, and souvenirs all cost extra.

Will your food and drink come from your hotel or from restaurants? What about tips?

How will you travel from place to place within your destination city?

Honeymoon Planning Ideas

For the Crafty Bride: put time into your Honeymoon schedule for browsing markets for crafting materials.

For the Thrifty Bride: sign up for newsletters from discount travel websites and wait for a killer deal to come along. Don't be thrifty when it comes to trip insurance - buy it!

For the Feisty Bride: go to a Travel Agent and say two words: ALL INCLUSIVE.

STICKY SITUATIONS

Subject	Stickyness	Possible Solution
Paying Parents	The Groom's parents are not able to pay for the rehearsal dinner or the Bride's parents won't be paying for the wedding.	• Follow convention on the invitations: the Groom's parents are the hosts of the rehearsal dinner, the Bride's parents are the hosts of the wedding, OR • List both sets of parents as hosts for the wedding and hosts for the rehearsal dinner, OR • Don't mention hosts.
	The parents expect to make decisions because they are paying for the wedding.	• Prepare. Before you sit down with the paying parents, make some of the major decisions with your fiancé. This can prevent conflict before it starts. Ask the parents upfront if they expect to weigh in on the decisions. • Compromise. Remind your mom that you are planning an *intimate* wedding and there is only so much room. If she insists, then just let her invite her hairdresser. • Use a *Top Three* system. You choose your three favorite options for the cake flavor and then let the paying person make the final call (or vice versa).
Ultimatums	*Do what I say or I won't pay/I won't come.*	• Seek counseling or mediation. Immediately.
Imbalance of Invitees	The Bride's list of invitees is much longer/shorter than the Groom's.	• Match your Circle of Invitees (see page 19). Are you inviting the same categories of people? • At the wedding, put out a sign of have the ushers ask guests to 'choose a seat, not a side.'
Adults Only	Guests with babies and small children may take it personally.	• Indicate Adults Only in the reception card, then reach out to the people with nursing babies and let them know that they are the exception to the rule, OR • Book a wedding venue that has a *cry room* (Hint: churches are more likely to have one), and ask the officiant to tell guests about it prior to the ceremony. At the reception, provide childcare and a place for kids to be entertained, away from the party.
Weird Gifts	A guest gifted you with something you've never even heard of, let alone registered for.	• If you can't say anything nice, just say *Thank You*. Never EVER tell someone that you didn't like a gift. • Return the gift discreetly. Don't ask the gift giver for the receipt or its store of origin, but look up the brand online to find its retailer. • If there's no way of knowing where it came from, then re-gift it, sell it, or give the unwanted gift to charity.
No Gift	A guest shows up empty-handed.	• Do nothing. Say nothing. A gift is not an entry fee. You invited your guests because you want their presence, not their presents.

DESTINATION WEDDING CONSIDERATIONS

COST

- Choosing to do a destination wedding can make it possible to save big on your out-of-pocket cost.
- To travel and stay in your wedding city is often cost prohibitive for your guests. Is that a good thing or a bad thing?
- The wedding couple and their parents must pay for much of the same expenses: venue, food, musicians, officiant, etc. The guests pay for their own travel and accommodations. If you choose an all-inclusive venue, then the food and drink are included in the guests' accommodation cost.
- Consider paying for your attendants' travel and/or accommodations.
- The honeymoon planning is done! Just stay longer than your guests. Request a room apart from the block of guests.

GUESTS

- A small attendance typically goes with a destination wedding, but you do not have to be shy with your invitations. The great thing about sending lots of invitations is that the invitees can feel welcome, even if they cannot attend.
- Save-the-Dates for a destination wedding need to go out EARLY, up to two years ahead of the wedding date, so your guests can make the necessary arrangements and save up.
- To facilitate your guests' travel, set them up with a travel agent.
- Regularly contact your guests (e-mail is fine) with updates about group rates, booking deadlines, itinerary, and destination-specific information.
- Let your attendees know that you don't need any gifts, just their presence.
- Go the extra mile (figuratively) to make guests feel more comfortable in the foreign language, culture, and weather.

FOREIGN POLICY

- Marriage license - each state and country has its own requirements for a marriage licence. They may include proof of identity, residency requirements, blood tests, and extra fees for foreigners. If there are too many hoops to jump through, you can always legally marry in your own town before you depart.
- Passports - you and your guests must allow plenty of time for the passport process. The passport office offers a rush option, but it's more expensive, and it is still slow. (Hint: Host a passport party for your bridal party, doing each other's hair and makeup so you all can look extra good for the passport photos. Paperwork done, no micro-managing).
- Travel visa - check to see if your destination requires special permission or paperwork.
- Vaccines - check to see if there are any recommended precautions for travel to your destination, especially for children.
- Jet lag - allow time in your itinerary for you and your guests to adjust to the new time zone.

PLANNING

- All-inclusive venues will speed up the planning process. A wedding planner may be on staff, which will allow you to choose from a few pre-determined options for each big decision - with opportunities to upgrade at extra cost. This person can also make recommendations for anything that is not offered onsite.
- There are scam artists who are looking for people in your situation. If something is too good to be true or makes you uncomfortable, proceed with caution.
- When you see things in person, some details - like the cake or the venue itself - may not be what you are expecting. Once you're there, there's only so much you can do to change it, but you can always choose to be happy anyway.

ATTIRE

- Your wedding clothes (and the wedding supplies that you bring with you) will have to fit in your luggage. Choose your gown silhouette and your Groom's level of fanciness with this in mind.
- Research the climate at your destination and plan accordingly. If it rains a lot, you won't want to walk across wet paving stones in stilettoes. A beach ceremony is no place for a long train (dragging all those lacy details over sand).
- Let your guests know how to pack for the weather and activities.

SCRAPBOOK PAGES

A PLACE FOR
MAGAZINE CLIPPINGS - SKETCHES - PHOTOS

SCRAP

BOOK

For the Groom*

* this (short) section can apply to the partner who is not taking the lead on the wedding planning, whoever that may be.

A Message to Grooms

It took a lot of guts to pop the question, and (like it or not) you opened a floodgate of roses, lace, and relatives. The proposal is just the beginning, and now follows the wedding planning. For many grooms, this time period is filled with activities they never knew existed and discussion topics they couldn't care less about. Here is your chance to practice effective communication with your future wife. This may include sharing your feelings (*I don't care what color ink goes on our invitations... oh wait, anything but purple*), setting boundaries (*this week, I can spend Thursday night doing wedding stuff with you*) and making compromises (*I can help you make that decision if you can narrow it down to three options*).

Don't be surprised if one day your Bride starts crying because the birdseed is sold out of in the color she wanted. That's your cue to listen, acknowledge that she has a lot on her plate, and help her to de-stress. See *Ways to Support Your Bride-to-Be* on page 94 for ideas.

When planning the wedding stops being fun, there are two phrases that grooms say all the time: *I just want to be married* and *marriage is just a piece of paper*. Sound familiar? Unless your fiancée is willing to go Las Vegas, there is no fast-forward button. Even then, you might want to have a party with your friends and family to celebrate (Hint: that is called a reception). As for the *just a piece of paper* sentiment, here are some examples of other pieces of paper: a one-hundred dollar bill, a driver's license, and a diploma (none of which come easy or get handed out for free).

This is going to be your wedding day, too. If you put your stamp on the wedding plans, then you will have more to enjoy when the day arrives. The *Groom's To-Do List* (page 94) is there to help you navigate the planning journey, not to set a limit (or place demands) on your part. A *Decision Checklist*, like the example on the following page, will help you to help the Bride with the important details. Remember that the goal is to be married, and everything else is meant to celebrate your love and your future together. Enjoy it!

Groom's Decision Checklist

(an example)

Stuff to Help Do/Decide	Decision Deadline	Budget	Date to do Research
❑ Set the Date	_____	_____	_____
❑ Invitations	_____	_____	_____
❑ Ceremony & Reception venues	_____	_____	_____
❑ Officiant	_____	_____	_____
❑ Marriage preparation course	_____	_____	_____
❑ Marriage license	_____	_____	_____
❑ Wedding consultant/coordinator	_____	_____	_____
❑ Music (wedding and reception)	_____	_____	_____
❑ Groom's Cake	_____	_____	_____
❑ Reception Booze	_____	_____	_____
❑ Groom's attire	_____	_____	_____
❑ Groomsmen attire	_____	_____	_____
❑ Boutonnieres	_____	_____	_____
❑ Passports & Vaccines	_____	_____	_____
❑ Honeymoon Accommodations	_____	_____	_____
❑ Honeymoon Airfare	_____	_____	_____
❑ Groomsmen gifts	_____	_____	_____
❑ Photography & Video	_____	_____	_____
❑ Transportation	_____	_____	_____
❑ Gift Registry	_____	_____	_____
❑ OTHER: _____	_____	_____	_____
❑ _____	_____	_____	_____
❑ _____	_____	_____	_____
❑ _____	_____	_____	_____
❑ _____	_____	_____	_____
❑ _____	_____	_____	_____
❑ _____	_____	_____	_____
❑ _____	_____	_____	_____

Groom's To-Do List

- ❑ Read over the Checklist (pages 3-9) and Shopping List (pages 12-16), so you can get an idea of the scope of what's to come.
- ❑ Tell your Bride which action items on the Checklist you want to be involved in or want no part of. Use the Example Groom's Checklist on the previous page or make your own.
- ❑ Choose a few of these things to take care of by yourself (i.e. booking the DJ, choosing the groomsmen's attire, or setting up tables for the Reception).
- ❑ Invite some people to be your Best Man, Groomsmen, Ushers, and VIPs.
- ❑ Speak to your parents about their expectations: who they would like invited, what traditions they would like upheld, and if they will contribute to the wedding budget.
- ❑ Schedule time with your Bride to work on the wedding plans, get registered for gifts, etc. (Hint: Support her in all things wedding, even if you don't share her enthusiasm).
- ❑ Plan the Honeymoon (see page 86). Sometimes the destination is kept a secret from the Bride.
- ❑ Follow through on everything you committed to do, and do it early. You'll have plenty to do the week before the wedding, you don't need to be playing catch-up as well.
- ❑ Prepare speeches/toasts for the rehearsal dinner and the wedding reception.
- ❑ Thank your Groomsmen at the Rehearsal Dinner with gifts, a shout-out during your toast, and/or a thank you note.
- ❑ Get a gift for your Bride (other than the wedding, her rings, and a honeymoon). Write a letter to her and send it to her dressing room with your gift, just before the wedding.
- ❑ At the reception, give a toast and raise a glass to your new Wife.

Ways to Support your Bride-to-Be

- Just listen... even if she makes no sense.
- Do not offer to cancel the whole thing so she won't have any more stress from wedding planning.
- Offer to help with the planning in some way.
- Surprise her with something relaxing (like a massage, going to happy hour, a night alone in hotel room, or going on a hike... depending on what recharges her).
- Never surprise her by working on a wedding project that you are unfamiliar with - there may be so more to it than you can imagine.
- A good old fashioned pat on the back goes a long way.

Groom's Search Terms

Groom Planning
Wedding Toast
Groomsmen Attire
Wedding Budget
Honeymoon Surprise
Groom Duties

Made in the USA
San Bernardino, CA
01 July 2019